Macs For Seniors

for
dummies

A Wiley Brand

Macs For Seniors

3rd edition

for
dummies®
A Wiley Brand

by Mark L. Chambers

for
dummies®
A Wiley Brand

Macs For Seniors For Dummies®, 3rd Edition

Published by: **John Wiley & Sons, Inc.,** 111 River Street, Hoboken, NJ 07030-5774, www.wiley.com

Copyright © 2016 by John Wiley & Sons, Inc., Hoboken, New Jersey

Published simultaneously in Canada

For general information on our other products and services, please contact our Customer Care Department within the U.S. at 877-762-2974, outside the U.S. at 317-572-3993, or fax 317-572-4002. For technical support, please visit www.wiley.com/techsupport.

Wiley publishes in a variety of print and electronic formats and by print-on-demand. Some material included with standard print versions of this book may not be included in e-books or in print-on-demand. If this book refers to media such as a CD or DVD that is not included in the version you purchased, you may download this material at http://booksupport.wiley.com. For more information about Wiley products, visit www.wiley.com.

Library of Congress Control Number: 2016946386

ISBN: 978-1-119-24550-6 (pbk); 978-1-119-24573-5 (ebk); 978-1-119-24572-8 (ebk)

Manufactured in the United States of America

10 9 8 7 6 5 4 3 2 1

Contents at a Glance

Table of Contents

Introduction

I s a Macintosh the computer for you? I can unequivocally answer "Yes!" Why am I so sure? Because Apple has been producing the best consumer computers and programs for many years now — desktops, laptops, and software that surpass anything else now offered on the market. (Yes, that includes other famous companies you've heard of, such as Dell, Microsoft, and Gateway.) Macs are designed to be easy and fun to use, and computing beginners will find that Apple has a knack for writing the best personal-computer software around.

Let me be honest: I'm not easily impressed when it comes to computers. As a cynical old computer programmer (and curmudgeon), I've used every version of Windows that His Gatesness has produced, including the latest, Windows 10. I've used many Mac versions all the way back to 1989. I'm very sure that you'll have the same great experience I've had using a Mac. Macs are just easy and fun!

The current operating system, OS X (now in version 10.11, called El Capitan), performs like a Ferrari and looks as good, too. And don't let that term *OS* throw you. That's just the name for the engine under the hood. See? Easy. (And the *X* in OS X is pronounced *ten*, not *ex*. Now you're in the know.)

The book you hold in your hands is written especially for seniors, using the *For Dummies* design. You'll find easy-to-follow and light-hearted step-by-step instructions for using the major features of both your computer and El Capitan. What you *don't* find in this book is wasted space or a bunch of intimidating computer terms. Everything is explained from the ground up, just in case you've never touched a computer, let alone one from Apple.

Foolish Assumptions

All you need to follow along with this book is a Mac running OS X version 10.11 (El Capitan). (A desk, good light, and mouse pad are all up to you.) Even if you have a Mac running an earlier version of

OS X, this book will still become a trusted friend, although some of the screenshots throughout the book will look a little different from what you'll see on your screen, and some things I talk about may not quite jibe. If you're at the point of buying your Mac — maybe you're standing in a bookstore right now! — go right to Chapter 1 for some helpful advice on your choices and options.

Here's the good news: You *don't* require any of the following:

>> **A degree in computer science:** Apple designed El Capitan and Macs for regular people, and I designed this book for people of various experience levels. Even if you've never used a Mac, you'll find safe waters here.

>> **A fortune spent on software:** Almost every program covered in this book is included with OS X El Capitan — and the size of this volume gives you a rough idea of just how complete El Capitan is! Heck, many folks buy Macs just because of the free software they get, such as iMovie and Photos.

>> **An Internet connection:** Granted, you can't do much with Apple Mail (email) without an Internet connection, but computers *did* exist before the Internet. You can still be productive with OS X without receiving buckets of spam (junk email). And if you already have an Internet connection, this book helps you connect and become familiar with the best of what's online!

TIP

I'm guessing that you probably do want an Internet connection (if you don't already have one). See Part 4 for help on getting online. I also recommend using a power strip with a surge-protection feature for powering your Mac, but that's your call, too.

About This Book

This book is organized in a straight-through, linear fashion, although you don't have to read it that way (and certainly not in one session). Having said that, you can certainly hop right to whatever chapter fits the bill for you. If you do go to a more advanced topic — or just need a refresher on something — I give you lots of signposts to related chapters where you can find more information.

The book is divided into parts, each of which covers a different area of Mac knowledge. You'll find parts on software, the Internet, and Mac maintenance, for example. And each chapter discusses a specific application, connection, or cool feature of your Mac. So feel free to begin reading anywhere or to skip chapters at will. I do recommend that you read this book from front to back, as you would any good mystery novel, but it's your choice. (Watch out, though. Oncoming spoiler: For those who want to know right now, Microsoft did it.)

If you've read any other *For Dummies* books, you know that they come with a helpful, simple set of conventions. Here's what you find in this book:

TIP

» The Tip icons in this book point out information you don't want to miss.

» When I ask you to type a command (tell the computer to do something) or enter information (such as your name or phone number) in a text field, the text appears in bold like this: **Type me.** Then you just press the Return key (on the keyboard) to send the command or enter the text. Easy.

» When I give you a set of menu commands to use in a certain order, they appear in the following format: Edit ⇨ Copy. In this example, you click the Edit menu and then choose the Copy menu item, in that order.

» Sometimes when you tell the computer to do something — like make a word bold — you can use keyboard shortcuts instead of using a menu and clicking things. Keyboard shortcuts look something like this: ⌘+B. You press and hold down the ⌘ key and then press B. (No need to press Shift to make a capital letter: Just press B or whatever.) You might also see three keys strung together, like this: ⌘+Option+down arrow. That just means to press and hold the first one, press and hold the second one, and then press the third one (in this case, to mute sound in iTunes).

» If I mention a specific message that you see on your screen, it looks like this: `This message is displayed by an application.`

Where to Go from Here

I have just a few recommendations on how to proceed from here:

» Whether you're thinking about buying a new Mac or your new Mac is still in the box unopened in your living room, start with Part 1.

» If you want help setting things up, start with Part 2.

» If you already set up your Mac and you're familiar with El Capitan basics, start with Part 3.

» If getting online and using email are your top priorities, start with Part 4. Just realize that you may need to go back through earlier chapters to set things up.

» If you want to know how to protect your Mac from the dangers of the world or need to do some maintenance, check out Part 5.

» There's also a cheat sheet! You can find it by visiting `www.dummies.com` and typing **Macs For Seniors For Dummies Cheat Sheet** in the search field.

» For all other concerns, use the index or check out the table of contents to jump directly to the chapter you need.

» I may update this book from time to time. If so, you can find those updates at `www.dummies.com/`.

A Final Word

I want to thank you for buying this book, and I hope that you find that this edition of *Macs For Seniors For Dummies* answers the questions you have along the way! With this fearless guide in hand, I believe that you and your Mac will bond as I have with mine. (That sounds some-what wrong, but it's really not.)

Always remember this as you make your way through this book or come back to it for help: *Take your time!* Finding out how to use your computer isn't a race, and if something doesn't go quite right, don't worry. You won't break anything, there are no stupid questions, and learning new things takes practice and a little patience. You don't have to be a graphic artist, professional photographer, or video edi-tor. With your Mac and its software by your side, you don't have to be! All you "have to be" is ready to have fun and learn.

1

Buying and Setting Up Your Mac

IN THIS PART . . .

Evaluating and buying Mac computers and software

Choosing the right location for your new Mac

Turning on your Mac for the first time

Navigating your Desktop with your mouse or trackpad

Creating and changing accounts and passwords

Chapter 1

Buying a Mac

Shopping for a Mac can leave you dazzled by a long list of features, functions, acronyms, and assorted hoohah. This chapter is here to help explain what to look for and why while you're shopping, especially if this is your first Mac.

The best part? I wrote it in common English, with the smallest amount of technobabble possible. (That's my job!)

In this chapter, I show you

» Tasks and work that your Mac can perform

» Differences between hardware and software

» Differences among the models in Apple's Mac computer line

» Features you should look for while shopping for a monitor

» Specifications you should look for when comparing the central processing unit (also known as the CPU — the computer's brain) and memory

Know What Your Mac Can Do

I would bet that you already know why you want a computer. You have an idea what you want to do with a Mac, but you may not know *all* the things you can do with a computer.

To help get you excited about owning a Mac, here's a (very) short list of only a few of the most popular uses for a computer these days. See whether any of these uses reflects what you want to do or you see any tasks that you want to learn more about:

» **The Internet:** You knew I would start with the web and email. Now you can also add online games, instant messaging, social media (like Facebook and Twitter), shopping, banking, and Internet radio and video streaming to the mix. The Internet literally expands in front of your eyes, and your Mac can be your doorway to the online world.

» **Digital media:** Whether your interest is photography, video, or music (making it or listening to it), your Mac comes with everything you need to get started.

» **Data collection:** If genealogy is your passion — or collecting baseball cards, or cataloging stamps — your Mac can help you enter, organize, and present your data.

» **Productivity stuff:** Oh, yes! Your Mac can work hard as well, with productivity programs such as Microsoft Office and Apple's productivity application suite (Pages, Numbers, and Keynote), along with online applications like Google Docs. Compose documents, create spreadsheets, and build professional-looking presentations on your Mac with ease.

This list offers only a few high points. The more time you invest learning about your Mac and the software that's available, the more you'll get from it.

Understand Hardware and Software

First-time computer owners often become confused about what constitutes *hardware* and what should rightly be called *software.* It's time to clear things up!

In the computing world, *hardware* is any piece of circuitry or any component of your computer with a physical structure. Your Mac's monitor is a piece of hardware, for example, as is your keyboard. So are the components you normally can't see or touch (the ones buried inside the case), such as your Mac's hard drive. And even your computer's case is technically a piece of hardware, even though it's not electrical.

Figure 1-1 illustrates a common piece of hardware: an Internet router that connects a DSL or cable Internet connection with a home network.

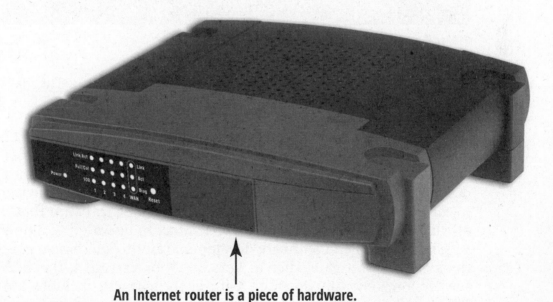

An Internet router is a piece of hardware.

FIGURE 1-1

The other side of the computing coin is the software you use. *Software* refers to programs (also called *applications*) that you interact with onscreen. Examples include a word processing application that displays your typing and a chess program that enables you to move pieces onscreen. **Figure 1-2** shows Apple's Photos image editor, a photo editing application that helps you see and organize digital photos.

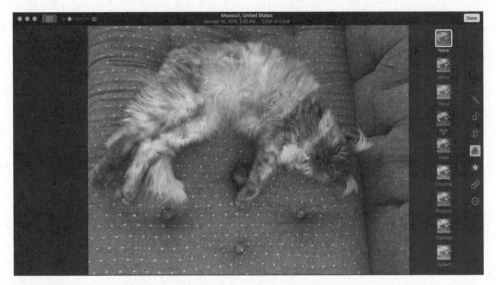

FIGURE 1-2

Essentially, computer hardware and software work together so that you can do various tasks on your computer.

TIP

When you hear folks discussing a software *upgrade, patch,* or *update,* they're talking about (you guessed it) *another* piece of software! However, the upgrade-patch-update program isn't designed to be run more than once; rather, its job is to apply the latest features, fixes, and data files to a piece of software that's already installed and running on your Mac, to update it to a new *version.* (Virtually all software developers refer to successive editions of their software, such as Version 1.5 or Version 3; the later the version, generally the more features the software includes.) In Chapter 18, you find out how to maintain your Mac with updates.

Choose a Desktop or Laptop

First, some quick definitions: A *desktop* Mac is designed to sit on your desk, and uses a separate monitor, keyboard, and mouse. Examples are the iMac, Mac mini, and Mac Pro. The iMac is a special case: It's an "all-in-one" computer, with the monitor and computer both housed in the same case to save space. However, the keyboard and mouse (or trackpad) still reside separately from the iMac's "picture frame" case.

On the other hand, a *laptop* Mac is portable. You can carry the whole package with you because laptops have a built-in keyboard, a trackpad (the square pointing device that takes the place of a mouse), and an attached monitor. MacBooks are laptop computers. Laptops are as powerful as most of the Mac desktop line, and MacBooks offer desktop-type features, such as high-resolution graphics, up to 15.4" screen displays, large hard drives, and wireless networking.

So should you buy a desktop or a laptop Mac? If portability is a requirement — maybe your job or your lifestyle demands travel — you want to opt for a laptop, such as a MacBook, MacBook Air, or MacBook Pro.

If you're sitting on the fence, and portability is a lesser requirement, I generally recommend getting a Mac desktop system, for these two important reasons:

» **MacBooks are more expensive than desktop Macs of similar capability.** My friend, you pay dearly for that portability. If you don't need it, jump to the desktop side of the fence. It's as simple as that.

» **Laptops cost much more to repair.** All Mac computers (both desktops and laptops) require the attention of a certified Apple repair technician if an internal component breaks. However, part of the MacBook portability stems from the computer industry practice of shoehorning all hardware onto one circuit board to save space. So if one piece malfunctions, you have to take apart (and perhaps replace) the whole thing, which isn't an easy (or inexpensive) task.

Bottom line, if portability isn't important, opt for a desktop — a Mac mini, iMac, or Mac Pro — depending on the processing power you need (as described in the following section) and the desk space you have available.

Know How Much Computing Power Is Too Much

Take a moment to consider which tasks your Mac will be used for — not only now, but also a year or two down the road. If you plan to try your hand at any of the following tasks, feel free to label yourself a power user:

» **High-resolution photography, audio and music production, or video editing:** If you want to edit high-resolution digital photography (images from a 24-megapixel camera, for example), record or edit professional audio, or do any type of video editing (including using the free iMovie application), you need a Mac with horsepower. Think of serious hobbyists or professional photographers, musicians, or videographers.

» **Running resource-hogging software:** The perfect example is Adobe Photoshop, a program you use to work with high-resolution images that demands the highest level of horsepower your Mac can deliver, along with requirements for more system memory (or RAM). Today's cutting-edge 3-D games also require a powerful Mac to run well.

If the preceding points apply to you, you need a powerful iMac desktop, Mac Pro desktop, or MacBook Pro laptop.

TIP

If you know the specific programs you'll be running, check the requirements for that software on the manufacturer's website or the program's packaging (typically, on the side of the box). That way, you can gain a better idea up front whether you need to invest in a more expensive, more powerful Mac Pro or MacBook Pro.

On the other side of the coin, these activities require less computing power:

» Surfing the web

» Sending and receiving email

» Keeping track of a large digital music library

» Using programs such as Microsoft Word and Pages for tasks such as creating documents

» Storing and sharing digital photos and videos of friends and family members

If the preceding tasks are more your speed, any Mac in the current product line would suit you, including the significantly less-expensive Mac mini or standard MacBook.

TIP

If you have a large library of digital audio and video — say, 120GB to 500GB — you should note that some MacBook models have a relatively small amount of storage, so you'll need an external hard drive to hold all that stuff.

Choose a Price Range

If you're working on a limited budget, and you want a new Mac computer (rather than having to search for a used machine), your choice becomes simpler. The least expensive Mac — the Mac mini — is no pushover, and it handles the Office and Apple productivity suite programs that I mention in the preceding section (with aplomb, even).

TIP

Part of the reason why the Mac mini is inexpensive is that it doesn't come with a keyboard, mouse, or monitor. Yup, you have to buy those items separately. (The same is true of the super-powerful Mac Pro.) If you're lucky, you can scavenge a flat-panel monitor, keyboard, and mouse from an old computer or from a friend who has spare computer hardware on hand.

The least expensive iMac also fits into a smaller budget, and it includes everything you need, including its built-in monitor. On the laptop side, the standard-issue MacBook provides plenty of punch for those same productivity programs.

Power users, you have few choices: If you're going to run top-of-the-line software that requires top-of-the-line performance, you're limited to the most expensive iMac, Mac Pro, or MacBook Pro. 'Nuff said.

Table 1-1 illustrates price ranges for each model in the Apple line as of this writing.

TABLE 1-1   ## Macintosh Computer Price Ranges

Computer Model	Best Suited For	Price Range	Pros & Cons
Mac mini desktop	Entry level to typical home computing	$499–$999	No monitor, keyboard, or mouse
iMac desktop	Midrange to power user	$1,099–$2,299	Built-in monitor
Mac Pro desktop	Power user	$2,999–$3,999	No monitor, keyboard, or mouse
MacBook laptop	Typical home computing	$1,299–$1,599	Fewer ports for external devices
MacBook Air laptop	Entry level to typical home computing	$899–$1,199	Least expensive MacBook
MacBook Pro laptop	Midrange to power user	$1,099–$2,499	Most powerful (and heaviest) MacBook

TIP

Apple controls its hardware prices quite closely, so you won't find a huge price difference between ordering directly from Apple.com (or an Apple Store) and from an independent store like Best Buy.

When you order a Mac from Apple.com, you can tweak these prices by a significant amount by using the Configure feature. You might save $200 on the price of an iMac by opting for less storage capacity, for example. (On the other hand, if you're looking to improve the performance of your pick, you may decide to spend more on a faster video card than the standard model sports.) See the later section "Compare Processors, Memory, and Hard Drives" for more information about these options. (Naturally, the more you can invest in your Mac's storage, memory, and processor, the longer it's likely to handle the applications and operating systems of the future.)

Select a Monitor

No matter how powerful your Mac may be, if it's hooked up to a low-quality monitor, you see only chunky, dim graphics. Not good. Hence this section, where I tell The Truth about the two most important specifications you should consider while shopping for a monitor: resolution and size.

TIP

If you decided on an iMac (desktop) or a MacBook (laptop), you can skip this section, because those computers have built-in monitors. Keep in mind, however, that you can hook up external (add-on) monitors to any Mac, so if you expand your system, you may want to return here.

>> **Resolution:** Your video system's monitor resolution is expressed in the number of pixels displayed horizontally and also the number of lines displayed vertically. (A *pixel* is a single dot on your monitor.) A 1024 x 768 resolution, for example, means that the monitor displays 1,024 pixels horizontally across the screen and 768 pixels vertically. (Any resolution less than 1280 × 800 is barely usable these days. Higher resolutions start at about 1440 × 900 and extend to the stunning 5120 × 2880 resolution of the latest 27-inch iMacs.)

TIP

The more pixels, the higher the resolution. And the higher the resolution, the more information you can fit on the screen, but the smaller that stuff appears, which I find to be a strain on my older (read: *wiser* and *more mature*) eyes. The good news is that higher resolutions make graphics look crisper.

Only you can determine the best display resolution. The decision is completely personal, like choosing a keyboard that feels "just right." While shopping for a monitor, try a wide range of resolutions at a local electronics store to see which one suits your optic nerves.

» **Size:** Monitors come in several sizes, starting at approximately 11 inches (for the most compact MacBook models). All monitors are measured diagonally, just as TVs are. You can easily find monitors that are 27 inches and even larger.

In general, the larger the monitor, the easier it is on your eyes. At the same resolution, a 19 inches monitor displays the same images as a 17 inches model, but the image is bigger and the details stand out more clearly.

For general desktop use, a 17 inches monitor is fine. If you prefer to view larger text and graphics, do graphics-intensive work for several hours at a time, or plan to do a lot of gaming, I would point you toward a 21 inches monitor at minimum. (As my editor says, picking out a monitor size is much easier if you visit your local electronics store and "stare to compare," just as you would when shopping for an HDTV. Check out which monitor sizes are easiest on both your eyes and your budget.)

TIP

And what about that old CRT (*cathode ray tube*) monitor that you once used with your PC? Is it worth rescuing? To be honest, I recommend that you get rid of a CRT monitor in favor of a flat-screen LCD or LED monitor. Older CRT monitors can't handle the high resolutions offered with today's Macs, and they use far more power than a modern LED monitor.

Compare Processors, Memory, and Hard Drives

When you hear Mac owners talk about the *speed* and *performance* of their computers, they're typically talking about one of four components (or all these components as a group):

» **System memory or random access memory (RAM):** The more memory your Mac has — and the faster that memory is — the better your computer performs, especially on *OS X El Capitan* (pronounced oh-ess-*ten*, not *ex*), which is the operating system on today's Macs. I'm sure that you've heard of Windows, the operating system used by virtually all home PCs. Well, El Capitan does the same job in the Apple world that Windows performs in the PC world.

» **Central processing unit (CPU):** Macs now use either an Intel Core i5/i7 processor or its faster cousin, the Xeon. A processor performs all the millions of calculations required for both your software and OS X to work. The speed of your processor is measured in gigahertz (gHz) — and, of course, the faster your processor, the faster your Mac performs.

TIP

Each *core* that's built into your processor provides a significant performance boost, so a quad-core processor is faster than a dual-core processor.

» **Hard drive space:** The higher your hard drive capacity, the more documents, programs, songs, and movies you can store and use. (Most current Mac laptops and desktops can be ordered with *solid-state drives,* which are lower in capacity but faster and more reliable than traditional hard drives.)

» **Graphics processing unit (GPU):** This item is the graphics chip used in your Mac's video hardware. The more memory allotted to your video chip and the faster it is, the smoother and more realistic your 3-D graphics are.

For a typical home Mac owner, a minimum of 4 gigabytes (GB) of RAM and a Core i5 processor should provide all the power you need. Power users shouldn't settle for less than 8GB of RAM and the fastest processor that Apple offers for your specific model. (Mac Pro owners can even opt for a monstrous 12-core system. Talk about supercomputing!)

Decide Which Software You Want

When you buy a Mac directly from Apple, you can immediately purchase a few Apple extras for your new system. I especially recommend the following two:

» **External DVD SuperDrive:** Virtually none of today's Macs have an internal DVD drive, so you can connect one to your Mac's USB port. Currently, the SuperDrive runs about $80. A DVD drive is a requirement for enjoying your library of DVD movies, and it comes in especially handy for creating audio CDs for your car's stereo system.

» **AppleCare:** AppleCare is the Apple extended warranty and service plan. I strongly recommend AppleCare for any MacBook owner because your laptop tends to endure quite a bit of road-warrior treatment while you're traveling. (Prices vary according to the type of computer.)

Buy Online or at the Apple Store

Should you spend your money online? In my opinion, the short answer is yes, because online shopping has two important advantages:

» **You don't need a nearby Apple Store:** Some of us aren't lucky enough to live within easy driving distance of an Apple Retail Store or Apple reseller, but Apple.com is open 24/7, and shipping is free for new Mac computers.

» **Apple.com is a premiere web store:** You can configure your Mac while browsing to save money or increase performance, so if you're interested in a custom configuration, the online store is the preferred method. Also, you can rest assured that Apple follows a strict privacy statement and offers secure encrypted shopping. That means your credit card information is safe.

You gain two major advantages by shopping in person, however: You can ask questions and receive answers from a trained salesperson before you buy, and you can drive away with that fancy box in your trunk (without having to wait a few days).

Chapter 2

Setting Up Your Mac

Remember the classic iMac advertisements that touted the one-plug approach to the Internet? The entire campaign centered on one idea: The Internet *should* be easy to use.

That's the Mac Way, and our good friends at Apple do their best to make sure that hardware and software work together as closely as possible. (Read about hardware and software in Chapter 1.) Their hard work means that you're left with as few configuration and technical details as possible while setting up your system. In this chapter, I cover the relatively few details you still *do* have to worry about.

In this chapter, I show you how to

» Find the perfect spot for your Mac and then unpack it

» Connect all the gizmos and doodads that came with your Mac

» Set up your account, as well as any additional accounts you need

Choose a Location for Your New Mac

If you choose the wrong spot to park your new Mac, I can *guarantee* that you'll regret it. Not all domiciles and office cubicles offer a choice, of course; you have one desk at work, for example, and nobody will hand over another one. But if you *can* select a home for your Mac, consider these important points:

» **Keep things cool.** Your new Mac is silent, but that superfast Intel processor generates heat. Make sure that the location you choose is far from heating vents and shielded from direct sunlight. If you're using a laptop, I also recommend a *cooling pad,* which elevates the base of your laptop to allow air to circulate underneath. (Some cooling pads even include a fan.)

» **Outlets are key!** Your computer needs a minimum of at least one nearby outlet and perhaps as many as three:

- A standard AC outlet (using a current adapter if you're traveling abroad, if necessary).

TIP

  Here's where a surge-suppressor strip or an uninterruptible power supply (UPS) unit comes in handy, providing multiple AC outlets from a single jack. At the same time, these strips provide protection against power surges while making it easy to turn off all your peripherals with a single ON/OFF switch while you're away on vacation.

- A telephone jack (if you have an external USB analog modem for connecting to the Internet)

- A nearby Ethernet jack (if you'll be connecting to a wired Ethernet network, a DSL modem, or a cable modem)

  If you prefer to send your data over the airwaves (and you have a broadband cable or DSL connection to the Internet), consider wireless networking for your Mac. Your local Apple reseller can offer an AirPort Extreme wireless base station that provides a wireless network with a shared Internet connection among all the computers in your home or office. (The Apple Time Capsule unit also acts as a base station, with the extra protection of a wireless backup drive.)

» **Don't forget the lighting.** In the words of moms everywhere, "You can't possibly expect to work without decent lighting! You'll go blind!" You need a desk lamp or floor lamp at minimum.

» **Plan to expand.** Allow an additional foot of space on each side of your Mac on your desk. That way, you have room for external peripherals, more powerful speakers, and an external keyboard and mouse if you need one.

Unpack Your New Mac

You're going to love this section, because the configuration of a Mac is a piece of cake. (Sorry about the cliché overload, but this really *is* easy.)

Follow these guidelines when unpacking your system:

» **Check for damage.** I've never had a box arrive from Apple with shipping damage, but I've heard horror stories from other people (who claim that King Kong must have been working for That Shipping Company).

Check all sides of the box before you open it. If you find significant damage, take a photograph (just in case).

» **Search for all the parts.** When you're removing those chunks o' foam, make certain that you check all sides of each foam block for parts snuggled therein or taped for shipment (including things like the power cable, keyboard, and your mouse or trackpad).

» **Keep all packing materials.** Do *not* head for the trash can with the original box and packing materials. Keep your box and all packing materials for at least a year, until the standard Apple warranty runs out. If you have to ship your computer to an Apple service center, the box, including its original packing, is the only way for your machine to fly.

TIP

Smart computer owners keep their boxes much longer than a year. If you sell your Mac or move across the country, for example, you need that box. *Trust me on this one.*

» **Store the invoice for safekeeping.** Your invoice is a valuable piece of paper indeed. Save the original invoice in a plastic bag, along with your computer's manuals, original software, and other assorted hoohah. Keep the bag on your shelf or stored safely in your desk, and enjoy a little peace of mind.

» **Read the Mac manual.** "Hey, wait a minute, Mark. Why do I have to read the manual from Apple along with your tome?" Good question, and here's the answer: The documentation from Apple might contain new or updated instructions that override what I tell you here, including some subtle configuration differences between Mac models ("*Never* cut the red wire — cut the blue wire instead" or something to that effect). Besides, Apple manuals are rarely thicker than a restaurant menu.

TIP

You can always download the latest updated manuals for Apple computers in electronic format from the Apple website at http://support.apple.com/manuals. *Adobe PDF format* is the standard for reading documents on your computer, and El Capitan (the operating system on your new Mac) can open and display any PDF document. I always keep a copy of the PDF manual for my MacBook Air on my hard drive, just in case.

Get Power

After your new Mac is resting comfortably in its assigned spot, you need to make that important first required connection: the power cable. Plug the cable into the corresponding socket on the Mac first and then plug 'er into that handy wall outlet (or surge protector, or UPS). Don't turn the computer on yet; you're not quite to that point.

Figure Out Ports

Before you make any connections between the outside world and your Mac, this is a good spot to cover the ports on your Mac. In computerspeak, a *port* isn't where the cruise ship docks; *ports* are those rows of holes on the sides of your computer. Each port connects a different type of cable or device, allowing you to easily add all sorts of functionality to your computer.

Here's a list of what you'll find and a quick rundown of what these ports do. These connections are for external devices and networking:

- » **USB:** Short for *Universal Serial Bus,* the familiar USB port is the jack-of-all-trades in today's world of computer add-ons. Most external devices that you connect to your Mac (such as a portable hard drive, scanner, and digital camera) use a USB port, and so does the iPhone, iPad, and iPod. Depending on the Mac model you're using, you can have up to four USB ports. All Macs except the MacBook include USB 3.0 support; the MacBook uses a new USB-C port instead of a standard USB 3.0 port.

- » **Thunderbolt 2:** The Thunderbolt 2 port is the new king among Mac ports. Thunderbolt 2 provides the absolute fastest performance for all sorts of external devices — everything from external hard drives to monitors.

- » **SDXC card slot:** With this handy port, your Mac can use the same SDXC memory cards as today's digital cameras. Things couldn't get much more convenient. Just pop the card out of your camera and insert it into your Mac, and you can open, edit, and save your digital photos without any time-consuming downloading through an old-fashioned cable!

 » **Ethernet:** All of today's desktop Macs include a standard gigabit Ethernet port, so your Mac is ready to join your existing wired Ethernet network. (Alternatively, you can go wireless for your network connection.) *Gigabit* indicates the speed of the network connection. Today's Macs can handle the fastest network speeds you're likely to encounter at your home or office, so feel free to be smug.

Apple designed the latest MacBooks to be wireless, so they don't have a wired Ethernet port built in. If necessary, you can add a USB or Thunderbolt Ethernet adapter to use a wired network port with your laptop.

 » **FireWire:** This port is the standard in the Apple universe for connecting external hard drives and DVD recorders, but it does double duty as the connector of choice for peripherals such as your digital video (DV) camcorder. (A *peripheral* is another silly technonerd term that means a separate device you connect to your computer, such as a camera or printer.) A small number of today's Mac computers have at least one FireWire 800 port onboard.

Oh, and don't forget the connections for external video and audio:

 » **HDMI connector:** Some Mac models allow you to send video to an HDMI-equipped monitor or high-definition TV.

 » **Headphone/optical output:** You can send the high-quality audio from your Mac beast to a set of standard headphones or an optical digital audio device, such as a high-end home theater system.

Access the Internet

If you have active Internet access or a local computer network, you also need to make at least one of the connections in this section.

For dial-up: If you get on the Internet by dialing a standard phone number, and your computer has an external El Capitan–compatible USB modem (a little box connected to your telephone line that makes all kinds of squeaks and skronks when you get on the Internet), you should make three more connections:

1. Plug your USB external modem into one of the USB ports on your Mac.

   The connector goes in only one way, which is a Good Thing.

2. Plug one of the telephone cable's connectors into your external modem.

3. Plug the other telephone cable connector into your telephone line's wall jack.

Your ISP (Internet service provider), such as AOL, should provide you account information and details on configuring your Internet settings for dial-up access.

High-speed Internet service: If your Internet connection is supplied by DSL or cable, the connection between your broadband modem and your Mac is likely through an Ethernet cable. If you're in an office or a school with a local computer network, you probably can connect by using your Mac's built-in Ethernet port. You make two connections:

1. Plug one end of an Ethernet cable into the Ethernet port on the Mac.

   An Ethernet connector looks like a telephone cable connector, but it's a little wider. If you can't locate the cable, yell for help from your network guru or cable/DSL provider. Remember that the current crop of MacBook models don't have an Ethernet port built in, although you can add one by buying a USB or Thunderbolt-to-Ethernet connector.

2. Plug the other end of the Ethernet cable into the Ethernet port from your network.

   Your network port is probably one of the following: an Ethernet wall jack, an Ethernet hub or switch, or a cable or DSL Internet router (or sharing device).

Use Keyboard/Mouse/Monitor

If your Mac arrives with a wireless mouse, keyboard, or separate trackpad, insert the batteries as shown in the setup guide, and always turn on the wireless devices before you turn on your Mac.

If you have a wired USB keyboard and mouse, on the other hand, a couple of connections are necessary:

1. Plug the USB connector from your keyboard into one of the USB ports on your Mac.

2. Plug the USB connector from your mouse into one of the USB ports on your keyboard.

Apple provides USB ports on most keyboards to prevent you from using up all your USB ports just for necessary gear.

As I mention in Chapter 1, some Apple models have their monitors built in, like the all-in-one iMac or the MacBook line of laptops. If you have one of these models, pat yourself on the back and do the Built-In Technology Dance, because your monitor is good to go.

If, however, you need to connect a monitor to your Mac mini or Mac Pro system, follow these steps:

1. Plug your monitor into a wall socket and turn it on.

   No, you won't see anything yet because you haven't yet powered on your computer.

2. Plug the HDMI cable from your monitor into the HDMI port on your Mac mini or Mac Pro. (If you have an older monitor that uses a DVI cable, you can order a DVI-to-Thunderbolt adapter from Apple and use your Mac's Thunderbolt port instead.)

HDMI and DVI cables are standard equipment with today's flat-panel monitors and high-definition TVs, but if you didn't get one with yours, you can pick up the proper cable at your local electronics store.

Use Your Mouse

Okay, you may have used a mouse on other computers, but if you're using a new Apple Magic Mouse 2, there's more you should know. The wireless Magic Mouse 2 from Apple (shown in **Figure 2-1**) is shaped somewhat like most mice you've likely used with other computers, but here are two major differences:

» **It has no buttons.** The entire surface of the mouse acts as the buttons! Press down with one finger anywhere on the top surface to left-click and on the top-right corner to right-click (the top-left corner for you lefties).

» **It recognizes multitouch gestures.** The surface of the mouse can also be used like a laptop's trackpad. In fact, you can opt to use an Apple Magic Trackpad 2 rather than a mouse with your desktop Mac. If you've used an iPhone, iPad, or iPod touch, you're familiar with many of these gestures already. If you're reading a long web page that covers multiple screens, for example, press your finger on top of the mouse and move your fingertip down to scroll down and display the additional text.

TIP

The Magic Mouse 2 uses an advanced laser optical system and doesn't require a mouse pad or special surface to work. If you'd rather not use your mouse on that expensive desk, though, a standard mouse pad might come in handy.

When you move your mouse across your desk, the mouse cursor moves along with it across your screen, in the same direction. OS X El Capitan is always aware of what your mouse cursor is on top of at the moment, allowing you to left-click, right-click, and double-click items to launch applications or turn things on and off. (More on this in upcoming chapters.) In the same fashion, moving your finger across the surface of a trackpad produces the same cursor movement on your screen, and you can tap with one or two fingers to left-click and right-click.

Turn On Your Mac and Run OS X Setup

After you press the Power button on your Mac — on either the side of the keyboard, or the front or back of the case — you hear the soon-to-be-familiar boot chime, and the Apple logo appears on your screen. A progress bar appears below the Apple logo to indicate that OS X El Capitan is loading.

In moments, you'll marvel at the liquid colors and intuitive controls that make up the OS X interface. Your Mac runs *El Capitan*, the latest version of the OS X operating system. (Most PCs run Windows as an operating system.) But wait — you're not quite done yet. OS X needs to be personalized for you, just like your iPhone or your car's six-way power seat. To personalize it, use the handy Setup Assistant, which automatically appears the first time you boot OS X El Capitan.

These assistant screens change periodically — and they're completely self-explanatory — so I won't march you through each one step by step. Here are a few tips that provide a bit of additional over-the-shoulder help while you're setting things up:

» **OS X speaks your language!** OS X defaults to U.S. formats and keyboard layouts. If you're outside the United States (or other English-speaking countries), though, rest assured that OS X does indeed provide full support for other languages and keyboard configurations. To display these options in the list boxes, click the Show All button at the bottom of the keyboard assistant screen.

» **Accounts are important.** OS X will ask you to create your *account,* which identifies you when you're using your Mac. OS X uses the name and password you enter to create your account, which you use to log in if you set up a multiuser system for several people. When you're creating your login account, *don't forget your password!* That's very important. And here's a big hint: Passwords are case-sensitive, so *THIS* is different from *this* or *ThiS.* Enter a password hint if you want, but don't make the hint easy to guess. *My first dog's name* is probably preferable to *Plays Seinfeld on TV.* Oh, and *never* write down your passwords; crib sheets work just as well for others as they do for you.

» **I need to change something.** You can click the Back button at any time to return to previous assistant screens. OS X, the bright child that it is, automatically saves your choices for you so that when you click Continue to return, everything is as you left it.

» **What about this extra stuff?** Whether to accept the news, offers, and related-product information from Apple is your decision. You can easily find this same information on the Apple website, however, so there's no need to engorge your email inbox.

» **It's good to make (network) connections.** If you're connecting your Mac to an existing network (or using an Internet router), click Yes when you're asked whether to use the configuration supplied by the existing server. (If you need to connect your Mac to a wireless network, you're also be given the chance to choose the network and enter the wireless network password.)

» **You need to have your Mail settings handy.** If you set up iCloud (Apple's online system for sharing data among your Mac, iPhone, iPod touch, and iPad), Mail sets up your free iCloud email automatically. Again, this is A Good Thing. If you're setting up an existing email account, make sure that you have all the silly settings, numbers, and names that your ISP supplied when you signed up. This stuff includes your email address, mail server variety, user account ID, password, and outgoing mail server. (El Capitan does the best it can to help you fill out this information automatically, but it can do only so much.)

Change Your Account Password

The El Capitan Setup Assistant helps you create your user account, a task that requires you to enter a username and choose a password.

Many folks like to change their passwords regularly. I should know; I'm one of them. It's especially important to be able to change your password if someone else discovers it — and that includes kids, who may not treat your files and documents with the respect they deserve!

TIP

I recommend that you change your account password at least once every six months for extra security.

You can easily change the password for your personal account. Follow these steps:

1. Move the mouse cursor over the Apple icon (🍎) in the upper-left corner of your El Capitan Desktop and then click that icon.

2. Click the System Preferences menu item that appears.

El Capitan displays the System Preferences window.

3. Click the Users & Groups icon to display the settings you see in **Figure 2-1**.

4. Click your account in the list on the left side of the Users & Groups pane.

5. Click the Change Password button to display the sheet you see in **Figure 2-2**.

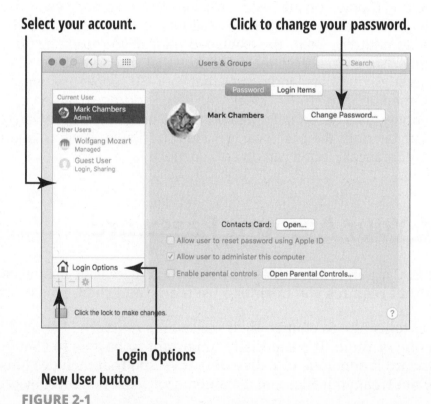

Select your account.   Click to change your password.

Login Options

New User button

FIGURE 2-1

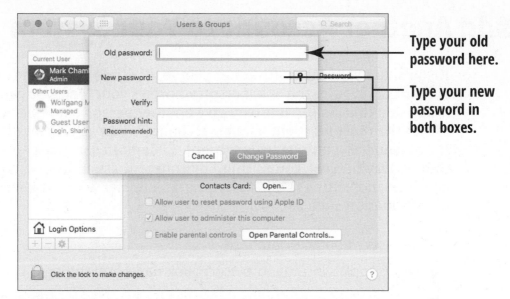

Type your old password here.

Type your new password in both boxes.

FIGURE 2-2

TIP

If you can't click the Change Password button because it's disabled — or "grayed out" — click the padlock icon at the bottom of the window. If prompted, type your old password to unlock the pane.

6. Type your old password and then press Tab on your keyboard to move to the next field.

7. Type a new password in the New Password text box and then press Tab to move to the next field.

8. Type your new password a second time in the Verify text box (to ensure that you didn't accidentally type it wrong the first time) and then press Tab to continue.

9. Type a short password hint that reminds you of the password you chose (just in case you forget it). Your hint should not be easy to guess, and it should *never* include your actual password!

10. Click the Change Password button.

11. Click the Close button in the upper-left corner of the System Preferences window to close System Preferences and save your changes (or press the convenient ⌘+Q keyboard shortcut).

Add Another Account to Your System

If you share your Mac with other people, it's time to add one or more accounts. (If you're the only person who uses your Mac, you can guilt-lessly skip this task.) "But why give another person a unique account, rather than just let them use my account?", you ask. Good question! If a person has a unique user account, El Capitan can track all sorts of things, leaving *your* computing environment (such as your Desktop and files and settings) blissfully pristine. A user account keeps track of information such as

» The user's Contacts database

» Safari (Apple's Internet browser) bookmarks and settings

» Desktop settings (including things like background images and screen resolutions)

» iTunes libraries, just in case that significant other buys his or her own music (sigh)

User accounts keep other people from accessing *your* stuff, and you can lock other accounts out of where-others-should-not-be, such as certain applications, Messages, Mail, and websites (including that offshore Internet casino site that your nephew favors).

Each user account you create also has a separate, reserved *Home folder*, where that person should store all his documents. Each user's Home folder has the same default subfolders, including Movies, Music, Pictures, Documents, and such. A user can create new subfolders within his Home folder at any time.

Here's one more neat fact about a user's Home folder: No matter what the account level is, most of the contents of a Home folder can't be viewed by other users. (Yes, that includes admin-level users. This way, everyone using your Mac gets her own little area of privacy.) Within the Home folder, only the Sites and Public folders can be accessed by other users — and only in a limited fashion.

A WORD ABOUT ACCOUNTS AND LEVELS

Get one thing straight right off the bat: *You* are the administrator of your Mac. In networkspeak, an *administrator* (*admin,* for short) is the one with the power to Do Unto Others, creating new accounts, deciding who gets access to what, and generally running the multiuser show. In other words, think of yourself as the monarch of OS X (the ruler, not the butterfly).

Next up is the *standard*-level account. Perfect for most users, this type of account allows access to just about everything but doesn't let users make drastic changes to El Capitan or create new accounts themselves.

Finally, the *managed* account with parental controls is a standard account with specific limits assigned by either you or another admin account. This account is useful for underage people in who might be using your Mac.

Remember: *Never* assign an account administrator-level access unless you deem it truly necessary. Standard accounts are quick and easy to set up, and I think they provide the perfect compromise between access and security. You'll find that standard access allows your users to do just about anything they need to do with a minimum of hassle.

"All right, Mark," you're saying by now, "enough pregame jabbering — show me how to set up new accounts!" Your Mac already has one admin–level account set up for you (created during the initial El Capitan setup process), and you need to be logged in with that account to add a user. To add a new account, follow these steps:

1. Click the System Preferences icon (as shown in the margin) on the Dock — the strip of icons at the bottom of your screen.

2. In the resulting System Preferences window, click the Users & Groups icon to display the Users & Groups pane (refer to **Figure 2-1**).

3. Click the New User button — the one with the plus sign at the bottom of the accounts list — to display the New Account sheet, shown in **Figure 2-3**.

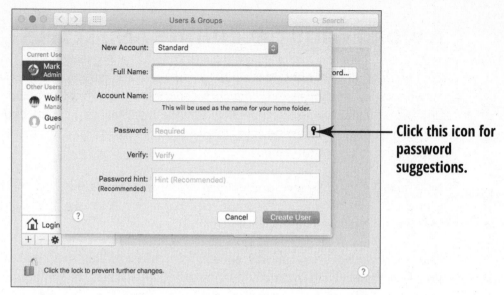

Click this icon for password suggestions.

FIGURE 2-3

TIP

If the New User button is grayed out, the Users & Groups pane is locked. You can toggle the padlock icon in the lower-left corner of most of the panes in System Preferences to lock (prevent) or unlock (allow) changes.

To gain access, do the following:

a. *Click the padlock icon to make changes.*

b. *If El Capitan prompts you for your admin account password (the account you're using), enter it.* (This password is the one you entered during El Capitan setup, when you created your personal user account.)

c. *Click OK.* You see a snappy animation as the padlock opens, and now you can click the New User button.

4. Click the New Account pop-up menu, and specify the account-level status:

- Choose Standard (unless the user should be assigned an Administrator or Managed with Parental Controls account).

- You should have only one or two administrator-level users, and your account is already an admin account.

5. Type the name that you want to display for this account in the Full Name text box, and press Tab to move to the next field.

TIP

El Capitan displays this name on the login screen, so behave! (Bob had only one letter *o*, the last time I checked.)

6. (Optional) Although El Capitan automatically generates the user's *short name,* for use in programs and for naming the user's Home folder, type a new one if you want; then press Tab again.

No spaces, please, and it's a good idea to use all lowercase letters for the short name.

7. In the Password text box, type the password for the new account, and press Tab to move to the next field.

I generally recommend a password of at least six characters, using a mixture of letters and numbers.

TIP

If you run out of password ideas, no problem! Click the key button (to the right of the Password text box) to display the Password Assistant, from which El Capitan can automatically generate password suggestions of the length you specify. Click the Suggestion pop-up menu or type directly in the Suggestion field, and El Capitan automatically adds to the Password field the password you generated. (Don't forget to commit the suggested password to memory!)

8. In the Verify text box, retype the password you chose, and press Tab again to continue your quest.

9. (Optional) To have El Capitan provide a password hint after three unsuccessful login attempts, type a short question in the Password Hint text box.

TIP

Keep in mind that from a security standpoint, password hints are taboo. (I *never* use them. If someone is having a problem logging in to a computer I administer, you had better believe that I want to know *why*.) If you do offer a hint, *keep it vague.* Avoid such hints as "Your password is the name of the Wookie in *Star Wars*." *Geez.* Instead, use something personal, such as "My first pet's name."

10. Click the Create User button.

The new account shows up in the list on the left side of the Accounts pane.

Switch between Accounts

After you create more than one account, your significant other has to reach his or her stuff, too. You can switch accounts in two ways:

» **Reboot or log off.** Click the familiar Apple symbol (🍎) on the menu bar at the top of the Desktop; it's in the upper-left corner. From the menu that appears, you can choose a command to restart your Mac (which shuts down your computer and reboots it) or log out (which presents the El Capitan login screen). On the login screen, a new person can enter his username and password.

» **Use Fast User Switching.** This feature allows another user to sit down and log in while the previous user's applications are still running in the background. This strategy is perfect for a fast email check or for skimming your eBay bids without forcing someone else completely off the Mac. When you turn on Fast User Switching, El Capitan displays the active user's name at the right end of the Finder menu bar.

To use Fast User Switching, you must turn it on from the System Preferences window. Follow these steps:

1. Click the System Preferences icon on the Dock (it sports several gears) and then click the now-incredibly-familiar Users & Groups icon to display the Users & Groups pane (refer to **Figure 2-1**).

2. Click the Login Options button.

   If the pane is locked, don't forget to click the padlock icon and type your account password to unlock it.

3. Select the Show Fast User Switching Menu As check box to enable it; then choose how the current user should be displayed in the menu bar by choosing the appropriate command from the pop-up menu.

   You can select the user's full name, short name, or account icon. The default setting (full name) is a good choice.

4. Click the Close button in the upper-left corner of the System Preferences window to close System Preferences and save your changes.

After Fast User Switching is turned on, follow these steps to use it:

1. Click the current user's name in the upper-right corner of the Desktop menu, as shown in **Figure 2-4**.

FIGURE 2-4

2. Click the name of the user who wants to log in.

El Capitan displays the login window, just as though the computer had been rebooted.

TIP

Because the previous user's stuff is still running, you definitely should not reboot or shut down the computer!

After the password is entered, you'll see the entire screen rotate, and the second user's Desktop appears. Spiffy! If you click the username on the menu again, you'll see that each logged-in user has an orange check mark.

3. To switch back to the previous user, do the following:

   a. *Click the username again on the Finder menu.*

   b. *Click the previous user's name.*

   For security, El Capitan prompts you for that account's login password.

If either user is finished with the Mac, that user can simply click the Apple menu and choose Log Out, and the other user can log back in and return to the tasks at hand.

Set Your Mac's Date and Time

Nothing's more irritating than a blinking 12:00 on a microwave or an alarm clock, and the same is true on your Mac. Personally, if I don't have the correct time, I get downright ornery. Luckily, El Capitan makes it easy to set your clock. In fact, if you have broadband Internet service, you can let your Mac set the time automatically!

Follow these steps to set your Mac's date and time:

1. Click the clock display on the menu bar at the top of your Desktop.

2. From the menu that appears, choose Open Date & Time Preferences to display the Date & Time pane.

3. Click the Date & Time tab at the top of the pane to display the settings you see in **Figure 2-5**.

4. Click today's date within the minicalendar to set the system date.

5. Click the field above the clock, and type the current time to set the system time.

   To set your Mac's time zone, click the Time Zone tab and then click your approximate location on the world map to choose a time zone. You can also click the Closest City pop-up menu and choose the city that's closest to you (and shares your same time zone).

6. Press the ⌘+Q shortcut to close System Preferences and save your changes.

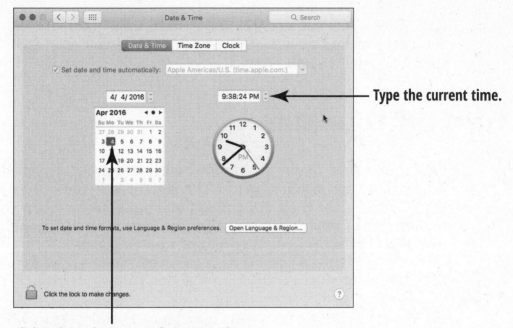

Type the current time.

Click today's date to set the system date.

FIGURE 2-5

As long as you have cable or DSL Internet access, the Mac can use an Internet time server to synchronize the time and date. Follow these steps:

1. Click the clock display on the menu bar at the top of your Desktop, and then choose Open Date & Time Preferences from the menu that appears.

2. Click the Set Date & Time Automatically check box to enable it, and choose from the pop-up menu a server that corresponds to your location.

TIP

Click the Clock button, and you can choose to view the time in text or icon format by selecting the Show Date and Time in Menu Bar check box. You can also optionally display seconds, AM/PM, and the day of the week; have the time separator characters flash; or use a clock based on 24 hours.

3. Click the Close button in the upper-left corner of the System Preferences window to close System Preferences and save your changes.

Bam! Now your Mac updates the system time automatically — and you're the technosavvy Mac owner! (You no longer even have to keep track of daylight saving time.)

Turn Off Your Mac

First things first. As the guy on the rocket sled probably yelled, "This is neat, but how do you stop it?" The Big Three — Sleep, Restart, and Shut Down — are the OS X commands that you use when you need to take care of other business. All three appear on the friendly Apple menu (🍎) in the upper-left corner of your Desktop.

Each option produces a different reaction from your Mac:

» **Sleep:** You don't need a glass of water or a bedtime story when you put OS X El Capitan to *Sleep,* which is a power-saving mode that lets you quickly return to your work later. ("Waking up" from Sleep mode is much faster than booting or restarting your computer, and it can conserve battery power on laptops.) To awaken your slumbering supercomputer, just click the mouse or press any key on the keyboard. MacBook owners typically put their laptops to sleep simply by closing the computer and wake the beast by opening it again (a neat trick when you carry your MacBook in a bag or backpack).

» **Restart:** Use Restart if your Mac suddenly decides to start thinking "outside the box" and begins acting strangely — if your USB ports suddenly lock up, for example, or your network connection no longer responds. Naturally, you need to save any work that's open. (Some applications and Apple software updates also require a restart after you install them.)

» **Shut Down:** When you're ready to return to the humdrum real world and you're done with your Mac for now, use the Shut Down option. Well-behaved Mac applications automatically prompt you to save any changes you made in open documents before the computer turns itself off (or restarts). If you configured your Mac with multiple accounts, you can shut down OS X El Capitan from the login screen as well.

2

Getting Started with Your Mac

IN THIS PART . . .

Using and customizing the El Capitan Desktop

Running programs, creating documents, and viewing files and folders

Using Finder windows, the Dashboard, and the Dock

Using the OS X Help system

Filling and emptying the OS X Trash

Chapter 3

Getting Around the Mac Desktop

You use the Desktop and the Finder window (two El Capitan screen elements) to take care of most of the chores that every Mac owner performs repeatedly. In this chapter, you explore basic El Capitan spell-casting using the Desktop and Finder windows.

I also introduce you to the Dashboard within El Capitan, where you can use all sorts of *widgets* — mini applications — to take care of common tasks like displaying dictionary definitions and today's local weather.

To do stuff with your Mac, you move among the Desktop, Finder windows, and programs. As you read this chapter, don't worry if you feel like there's a piece you're not quite "getting." If you hang in there until the end, you'll be able to

» Open and close windows.

» Find important features.

» Move around the interface with ease.

Tour the Desktop

Your Mac Desktop is comparable to your physical desk: It holds the most important elements in a convenient view, ready when you need them. The Desktop includes the following elements (most of which are shown in **Figure 3-1**):

» **The Finder menu bar:** From here, you can give commands to the Finder. (You give the Finder lots of commands as you use your Mac.) I talk about the Finder in the next section.

» **The Apple menu:** Click the Apple icon at the left side of the Finder menu bar, and you'll find a number of menu commands that affect the entire system. Here's where you can access the documents and applications you've recently used, restart or shut down your Mac, and display information about your computer.

» **The Dock:** The Dock keeps at the ready the icons you use most often. You use these icons to launch programs or open files, as I explain in the section, "Open and Switch Programs from the Dock," later in this chapter. When you begin using your Mac, the icons you see are defaults, which Apple has preset for you. As you use your Mac more and more, though, you may decide to customize the Dock with the icons that *you* use most often.

» **The icon representing your hard drive:** All Macs have at least one internal drive, which is the storage device for all the data you want to save permanently. (If you add external drives, they may also appear on your Desktop as separate icons.) You can always double-click the drive icon to open a Finder window and display your files and folders.

» **Icons for files and folders you decide to park on the Desktop:** A new Desktop is similar to a new desk: It starts off pretty clean. You can keep files on your Desktop in the same way you can pile papers on your desk. You're generally better off, though, organizing files into folders so that you can find them easily. In fact, El Capitan is already equipped with default folders for stuff like photos and music. You find out more about working with files and folders in Chapter 5.

Apple menu   Finder menu   Hard drive icon

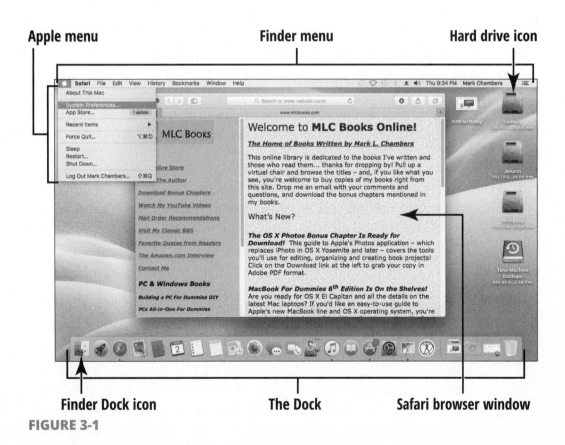

Finder Dock icon   The Dock   Safari browser window

FIGURE 3-1

» **Any open Finder and program windows:** *Windows* are contain-ers in which you interact with files or programs. Right now, you just need to know that windows appear on your Desktop. The next section explains how to open a Finder window, and later sections in this chapter explain how to run programs to open their windows, as well as how to work with those windows.

Discover the Finder

When you need to see the contents of your hard drive or copy items from one location to another, you open a Finder window. In other words, the Finder is the starting point for many of the tasks you perform with your Mac. Here are ways to open a Finder window:

» The easiest way is to double-click the Mac's hard-drive icon on the Desktop (refer to Figure 3-1).

» Alternatively, click the Finder icon on the Dock. Figure 3-1 illustrates the Dock with the rather perspective-crazy Finder icon on the far-left side. Is that icon supposed to be one face or two faces? I'm still confused, and I've been using the Mac since 1989.

TIP

The Finder is always running, so the Finder menu bar is *always* available — and you can always switch to it, even when several other applications are open and chugging away. If you ever need to return to the Finder, just click outside any window border (on any empty portion of the Desktop).

Use the El Capitan Icons

Icons are more than little pictures. And because these graphical symbols truly are representations of the components of your OS X system, they deserve a section of their own. In fact, you'll encounter icons everywhere: on your Desktop (as you already know), as well as on the Dock and in Finder windows. OS X also uses icons to represent the various hardware devices on your computer, including your

» Internal drive

» CDs or DVDs (if one is loaded)

» External drive connected by USB or Thunderbolt cable

You get the idea. Just double-click a hardware icon to display the folders and files it contains, as you do with your hard drive.

TIP

For complete details on what any icon is, what it represents, and what it does, click the icon once to highlight it and then press ⌘+I. This key combination opens the Info dialog. (In **Figure 3-2**, I'm displaying the Info dialog for my iMac's primary internal hard drive.) The Info dialog tells you what kind of item you've selected, where the item it represents is located, and how big the file is (if applicable). You also see a version number for applications — a handy way of quickly determining which version of a program you're running — and when the file was created and last modified.

I cover file and folder icons in Chapter 5.

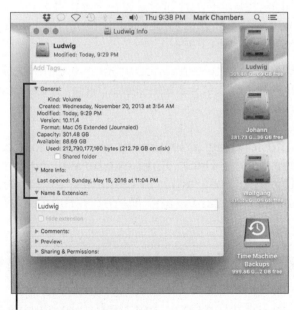

Find details about an icon.

FIGURE 3-2

Open and Switch Programs from the Dock

The Dock couldn't be any easier to use — and I *like* easy. The following steps walk you through basic Dock tasks and navigation. Hint: You can have more than one program open at a time. (Sweet!)

1. Click a program icon on the Dock to run a program. The program window opens. (Note that some programs you run from the Dock don't open a window, such as the Dashboard. Almost all programs, however, display a window.)

TIP

   Several programs appear on the Dock by default, such as Safari, the App Store, and iTunes.

2. Click a different icon on the Dock, and watch as another window opens. This second window covers the window you opened in Step 1 — but that's okay.

3. Click the icon that you clicked in Step 1 to move the first window to the front. (You can also click any part of the window that's peeking out — if it is — but you won't always have that option.) Now you see the window you opened in Step 1 again.

4. You can continue switching between windows, or even add a third, until you get the hang of it or just get bored watching the windows dance around on your screen.

TIP

Running a program and loading a document are the most common functions you use on the Dock. Find out how to customize the Dock with your favorite programs, documents, and more in the section "Add Favorite Programs (and More) to the Dock."

Run Programs from Your Internal Drive

You can start a program from the Dock, but that's not always the best way to start a program. This list describes a few more handy ways you can launch a program from your internal drive:

» **Use Launchpad.** See the rocket-ship icon on the left side of the Dock, as shown in Figure 3-1? (It always reminds me of the spaceships from the Flash Gordon movie serials.) Click the rocket icon to display El Capitan's Launchpad, where all your program icons hang out. If you've used an iPhone or iPad in the past, you'll recognize this scrolling display immediately. Just click a program icon to run that program, and Launchpad disappears.

TIP

If your Launchpad stretches over multiple screens, you can click anywhere on the Launchpad background and drag to the left or right to display additional icons.

» **Navigate to the corresponding program folder.** Although this solution isn't as quick or elegant as Launchpad, you can always use the Finder window to locate and run a program. Double-click the internal drive icon on your Desktop (refer to Figure 3-1) and then double-click the folder (and subfolders, if necessary) that contain the program. After the program icon is displayed in the Finder window, double-click it to run the program. To run Chess, for example, which isn't on the Dock, you double-click the internal-drive icon on your Desktop and then double-click the Applications folder to display the Chess icon. Now you can double-click the Chess icon to play a game.

» **Double-click a document or data file that's "owned" by the program.** Double-click an MP3 audio file to open iTunes, for example. You find out more about working with files in Chapter 5.

» **Double-click an alias you created for the program.** An *alias* is nothing more than a handy shortcut to something else, like a folder. For tips on using an alias, see Chapter 5.

Add Favorite Programs (and More) to the Dock

In terms of importance, the Dock ranks right up there with the command center of a modern nuclear submarine. For that reason, it had better be easy to customize, and naturally, OS X doesn't let you down.

The Dock is a convenient way to keep handy the stuff you use most often: the programs you run the most, and even folders and websites that you open many times every day.

You might be satisfied with just the icons that Apple places on the Dock. Or you can easily customize the Dock by adding your own applications, files, and folders there:

TIP

» **Add any program to the Dock.** Add a program to the Dock when you need to run it often and you'd rather not have to locate it in Launchpad every time! If the application is already running, you can simply right-click the icon in the Dock and choose Add to Dock from the menu. If the application isn't currently running, however, use a Finder window to locate the program (as I describe in the previous section). Then click and drag its icon into the area on the *left* side of the Dock (to the left of the solid line that appears on the Dock). You know when you're in the proper territory because the existing Dock icons obligingly move aside to make a space for it.

Don't release the mouse on the right side of the solid line on the Dock. Attempting to place an application on the right side of the Dock sends it to the Trash (if the Trash icon is highlighted when you release the button). If you make this mistake, see Chapter 5 for tips on retrieving your application. You don't want to empty the trash in this case, but you do find the steps you need to restore the file in that section.

» **Add a file to the Dock.** When you're continually opening a particular file to make additions or changes (such as on your budget spreadsheet), it's handy to have that file on the Dock. You can add individual file icons to the Dock by dragging the icon into the area to the *right* side of the Dock (to the right of the solid line). Attempting to place a document to the left side of the Dock opens an application with the contents, which usually doesn't work. Again, the existing Dock icons move aside to create a space when you're in the correct area. You can drag icons on the Dock to rearrange them, too.

TIP

Chapter 5 explains how to work with files and folders, including how to find a file's icon so that you can add it to the Dock. For now, just know that you have the ability to do so.

» **Add several files or a folder to the Dock.** El Capitan uses the Stacks feature, which I discuss in the next section. Stacks allows you to add multiple files (or the contents of an entire folder) to the Dock.

» **Add a website link.** You can drag any website page address (commonly called a *URL,* or Universal Resource Locator) from Safari (your web browser) directly to the area to the right of the Dock. Then clicking that icon automatically opens your browser and displays that page.

» **Remove an icon from the Dock.** If you add enough icons to the Dock, the icons get downright tiny and hard to see. To prevent this, it's a good idea to remove icons that you don't need and keep your Dock svelte (so that you can add more items later). Close the program that uses the item (if necessary) and then click and drag the icon off the Dock. You see a rather silly (but somehow strangely satisfying) animated cloud of debris, and the icon is no more. (Alternatively, you can remove an icon by right-clicking the icon in the Dock and choosing Options ➪ Remove from Dock.) Note, however, that the original application, folder, or volume is *not* deleted; just the Dock icon itself is permanently excused.

Stack Files and Folders on the Dock

Stacks are groups of items (documents, applications, or folders) that you want to place on the Dock for convenience — perhaps the files needed for a project you're working on or your favorite game applications. Right now, I have on my Dock a stack that holds all the project files I need for the book I'm now writing. A stack can be temporary, and you can remove it from the Dock as you do any other icon (as I demonstrate in the preceding section), or it can be a permanent addition to the Dock.

» **To create a stack:** Just select and drag to the right side of the Dock the group of items you want to include. As always, the Dock opens a spot on the right side of the Dock to indicate that you're in the zone.

» **To display the items in a stack:** Click it.

  • *If the stack holds relatively few items,* they're displayed in a cool-looking arc (shown in **Figure 3-3**), and you can click the item you want to open or launch.

Items in a stack

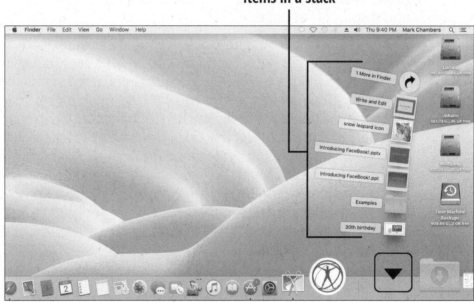

FIGURE 3-3

  • *If the stack is stuffed full of many items,* the stack opens in a grid display, allowing you to scroll through the contents to find what you need.

» **To remove a stack from the Dock:** Right-click the Stack icon and then choose Remove from Dock from the menu that appears. Alternatively, just drag that sucker right off the Dock.

TIP

Apple provides two stacks already set up for you. The Downloads folder, situated next to the Trash, is the default location for any new files you download from the Internet by using Safari or receive in your email. El Capitan bounces the Downloads Stack icon to indicate that you received a new item. Chapter 14 introduces you to web browsing with Safari, and Chapter 15 walks you through downloading files from an email. The second stack is the Documents folder, the location where most El Capitan applications (like Pages, TextEdit, and Preview) save the documents you create.

Change the Dock Size and Location

You can change the size of the Dock directly from the Desktop! Increasing the Dock's size can make it easier to see, and decreasing its size can make room for viewing other items onscreen. Follow these steps to change the size of the Dock:

1. Click the System Preferences icon on the Dock (which carries a gear symbol).

2. Click the Dock icon in the System Preferences window.

3. Click and drag the Size slider to reduce or enlarge the Dock.

You can also set Dock icons to grow larger whenever you hover your cursor over the Dock. The magnification feature can make the Dock icons easier to see. When magnification is turned on, the icons in the Dock grow *really* big. Check out the somewhat-oversize icons in **Figure 3-4**.

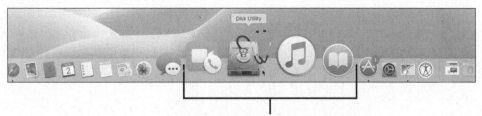

Magnification changes the icon size.

FIGURE 3-4

Follow these steps to change the magnification settings:

1. Click the System Preferences icon on the Dock.

2. Click the Dock icon in the System Preferences window.

3. Click the Magnification check box to toggle icon magnification on and off.

4. If you want to adjust the amount of magnification, you're in luck. Drag the Magnification slider to the right to increase the size of the magnified icons.

5. While you're here, you can adjust the hiding feature or the location of the Dock. Here's how these options work:

   • **Hiding:** Click the Automatically Hide and Show the Dock check box to toggle the automatic hiding of the Dock. With hiding on, the Dock disappears off the edge of the screen until you move the cursor to that edge. (This feature is helpful if you want to make use of as much Desktop territory as possible for your applications.)

   You can press ⌘+Option+D to toggle Dock hiding on and off from the keyboard.

   TIP

   • **Position:** Click one of three choices (Position on Screen Left, Bottom, or Right) to make the Dock appear on the left, bottom, or right of the screen, respectively.

Empty the Trash

As you work with your Mac to create files and folders and perform other tasks, it can become cluttered. Eventually, you want to delete some items, as I explain in Chapter 5 (which focuses on working with files and folders). From time to time, you may want to empty the Trash (the electronic bin on the Dock where deleted items are deposited) so that your deleted items aren't occupying space that you can use for other things. When you're compelled to take out your Mac's trash, follow these steps:

1. Click the Trash icon on the Dock to open the Trash.

2. Check the Trash contents to make absolutely sure that you want to delete them. You can retrieve files from the Trash, as I explain in Chapter 5, but you can't retrieve those files after you empty the Trash.

3. Click the Empty button at the top-right corner of the Trash window (or choose Finder ⇨ Empty Trash). This decision is all-or-nothing, so make sure that you're ready to delete.

TIP

For an extra level of security, you can choose Finder⇨Secure Empty Trash. El Capitan securely erases the contents of the Trash so that even a dedicated Mac technician couldn't recover anything!

Display the Dashboard and Widgets

One of El Capitan's most popular features is the *Dashboard,* which you can use to hold widgets and display them at the click of a button. (Okay, I know that sounds a little wacky, but bear with me.) *Widgets* are small applications that typically perform only one function. The Dashboard comes complete with a calculator, clock, weather display, and quick-and-simple calendar widgets. **Figure 3-5** illustrates the Dashboard in action.

TIP

Dashboard is turned off by default in El Capitan. To enable the feature, open the System Preferences window, click the Mission Control icon, click the Dashboard pop-up menu, and then choose As Space. Click the Close button at the upper-left corner of the System Preferences window to close the window and save your changes.

To display and customize your Dashboard display, follow these steps:

1. Press F12 to display your widgets, ready for you to use. (Note that some third-party keyboards may use another key for Dashboard.)

2. To add a widget to your Dashboard, click the Add button (which bears a plus sign, naturally) in the lower-left corner of the Dashboard screen. The Dashboard displays your current widgets.

3. You can click a widget icon to add it to your Dashboard, and you're returned to your Dashboard screen. (For more information on downloading widgets, check out Chapter 12. You'll find a huge number of widgets to download on the Apple website.)

4. To rearrange the widgets that are already populating the Dashboard, click and drag them to the spots you want.

5. When you're done with your widgets, press Esc or click the arrow at the lower right of the screen to return to the El Capitan Desktop.

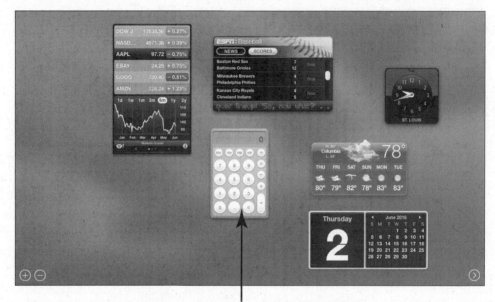

Calculator is one widget on the Dashboard.

FIGURE 3-5

Search Your Mac with Spotlight

The *Spotlight* feature lets you search your computer as quickly as you can type. You can use Spotlight to quickly search your Mac for documents, contacts, Mail messages, folders, and drives that your Mac can access. Spotlight can also search websites on the Internet. To search for items with Spotlight, follow these steps:

1. Click the magnifying-glass icon in the Finder menu. El Capitan displays the Spotlight search box (see **Figure 3-6**).

Search for a term.

FIGURE 3-6

2. Simply begin typing. Matching items appear below the Spotlight box as soon as you type, and the search results are continually refined while you type the rest of your search terms. Check out my tips and shortcuts for typing search terms a little later in this section. You can see a preview of the contents of any item by clicking that item.

TIP

The 20 most-relevant items are grouped into categories directly on the Spotlight menu, including Messages, Suggested Websites, Definition, Documents, Folders, Images, and Contacts. Spotlight takes a guess at the item that's most likely what you're looking for and presents it in the special Top Hit category, which always appears first.

3. If you don't find what you're looking for in the search results, try again. To reset the Spotlight search and try typing different text, press the Esc key. (You can also press Backspace to reach the beginning of the text box, but that method is a little less elegant.)

4. To open the Top Hit item like a true El Capitan power user, just press Return. (Folks, it doesn't get any easier than that.)

5. To open any other item, you can double-click it to

- *Run it* if the item is a program.

- *Open it in System Preferences* if it's a setting or description in a Preferences pane.

- *Open it within the associated program* if the item is a document, website, or data item.

- *Display it within a Finder window* if the item is a folder.

Any text string is acceptable as a Spotlight search. Here's a short list of the common search tips I use every day:

» **To find contact information:** Enter any part of the names or address. Because Spotlight has access to the El Capitan Contacts application, you can immediately display contact information by using any portion of a name or address.

» **To find an email message:** Type the sender's address or any unique word or phrase you remember from the message. If you need to open a specific email message, but you'd rather not launch Mail and spend time digging through the message list, enter the person's email address or any text string contained in the message you're looking for.

» **To display a file or folder name in the results list:** Type it. This is the classic search favorite. Spotlight searches your entire system for that file or folder in the blink of an eye.

» **To find out how to adjust System Preferences:** Type a keyword for the item you want to adjust. Now things start to get *really* interesting! Type the word **background** in the Spotlight field, for example. Some of the results are System Preferences panes! That's right — every setting in System Preferences is referenced in Spotlight. (The Software Update pane contains the word *background,* and the Desktop *background setting* is in the Desktop & Screen Saver pane in System Preferences.)

» **To search web pages:** *Whoa.* Stand back, Google. You can also use Spotlight to search web pages, as well as pages you recently displayed in Safari!

TIP

Here's another favorite time-saver: You can display all the files of a particular type on your system by using the file type as the keyword. To provide a list of all images on your system, for example, just use *images* as your keyword. The same goes for *movies* and *audio*.

View the Finder in Icon View

The default appearance of a Finder window in OS X uses the familiar large-format icons that have been a hallmark of the Macintosh operating system since Day One. This view, *Icon view*, is shown in **Figure 3-7**. You can display the contents of a Finder window in Icon view by clicking the Icon View button on the Finder window toolbar.

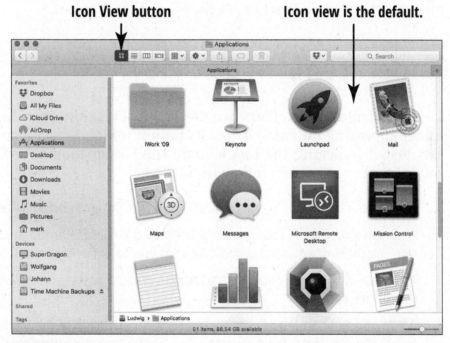

FIGURE 3-7

Using Icon view has these advantages:

> » **Items are larger in Icon view.** Items are easier to recognize in this view than in List or Column view.
>
> » **Dragging and dropping can be easier.** Copying and moving items from one window to another is often more convenient when you're using larger icons.
>
> » **Selecting multiple items can be easier.** Because of the size of the icons, you might find it easier to select more than one item in a Finder window while in Icon view.

TIP

You don't have to use Icon view. (In fact, most El Capitan power users whom I know consider Icon view rather inefficient and slow.) The next few sections in this chapter cover other ways to view items in the Finder. In addition to Icon view (refer to Figure 3-7), OS X offers List, Column, and Flow views.

List Finder Items in List View

List view displays the folders in a hierarchical fashion, with each sub-folder appearing indented below its parent folder. You can change to this view by clicking the List icon on the Finder toolbar. To display the contents of a folder, follow these steps:

1. Click to select a drive in the Devices list in the Finder window sidebar.

2. Click the small, right-facing triangle next to the folder name. The triangle rotates downward to indicate that you've expanded the folder.

   Alternatively, double-click the folder icon to display the contents in the Finder window.

3. If you need to display the contents of a *subfolder* (a folder stored inside the original folder), click the triangle next to the subfolder name to expand it and display the subfolder's contents.

4. To collapse the contents of the folder, click the small triangle again; it rotates to face the right.

Figure 3-8 illustrates the same Finder window in List view.

List View button

List view displays views hierarchically.

FIGURE 3-8

See Items in Column View

This view is my favorite — thanks, Apple! It's efficient and fast as all get-out. **Figure 3-9** shows the same window in Column view, in which the drives on your OS X system are displayed on the left. Each column on the right represents a lower level of subfolders. You switch a Finder window to Column view by clicking the Column View button on the Finder window toolbar.

To navigate in Column view, follow these steps:

1. Click the drive in the Devices list in the Finder window sidebar.

2. Click to select a folder in the first column on the right to display its contents. To display a subfolder's contents, click the subfolder's icon.

The contents appear in the next column to the right. When you "drill down" deeper, the columns shift automatically to the left.

When you click to select a file or program (rather than a folder), the Finder displays a preview and a quick summary of the selected item in the rightmost column.

Column View button

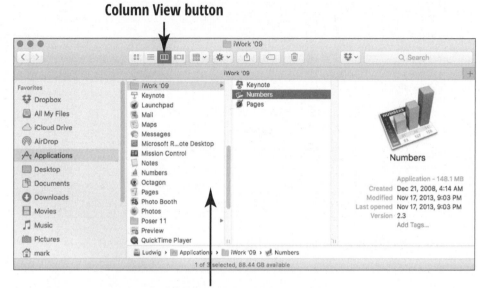

Column view displays folders and subfolders.

TIP

Each column has its own individual scroll bar (for those *really* big folders), and you can drag the column handle at the bottom of the separators to resize the column width to the left. When you hold down the Option key and drag a column handle, all columns are adjusted at one time.

Surf Items in Flow View

In Flow view, shown in **Figure 3-10**, each document or item is showcased in a preview pane (and with an accurate thumbnail, if possible). You can display a Finder window in Flow view by clicking the Flow View button on the Finder window toolbar.

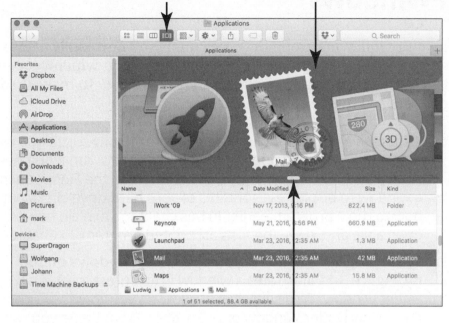

Flow View button   **Flow view displays each file in a preview pane.**

Scroll the preview pane.

FIGURE 3-10

Here are some other tricks to using Flow view:

» **Resize the preview pane.** Say you need more room in the file list. You can resize the preview pane by dragging the three-line handle on the bottom edge of the pane.

» **Expand and collapse.** You can expand and collapse the folders in Flow view just like you do in List view, using the rotating triangles.

» **Scroll the preview pane.** You can click the scroll buttons or drag the scroll bar below the preview pane to move through the contents of your drive in quite a classy visual display.

Open Windows

If you're following along in this chapter, you now know a few ways to open windows. But this section focuses only on window-opening. If you want something to open but aren't sure how to make it so, these pointers can help:

» **Windows are generally opened automatically.** Usually, a window is opened by an application (when you first run it or it needs to display a document) or by OS X itself (when the Finder opens a window to display the contents of your hard drive). I explain how to run a program earlier in this chapter. I explain how to open a file and, thus, the file's associated program, in Chapter 5.

» **Some programs even let you open new windows on the fly. Figure 3-11** illustrates a window in its purest form: a new Finder window. To display this window on your own Mac, choose File ⇨ New Finder Window or press ⌘+N. From there, you can reach any file on your Mac or even venture to the Internet.

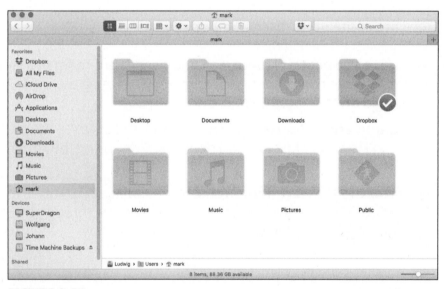

FIGURE 3-11

TIP

The Command key has on it both the word *Command* and a rather strange-looking symbol (⌘) that I often call the "spirograph."

Use Mission Control to Switch Windows

One of the neatest El Capitan features, aptly named Mission Control, is shown in **Figure 3-12**. If you have several windows open, Mission Control is a helpful way to find the one you want. Here's how the feature works:

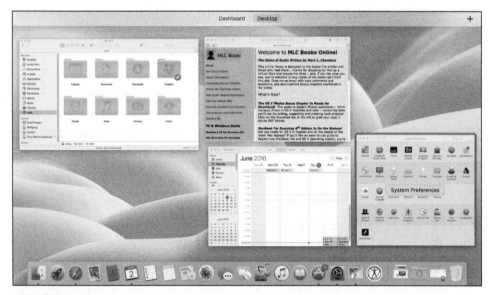

FIGURE 3-12

» Press F3 to show *all* open windows using Mission Control, grouped by application; then click the one you want.

TIP

Your Mac keyboard includes *function keys* (marked F1 through F12). These keys are generally used to perform specific actions within El Capitan and many applications. The function keys appear at the top of the keyboard.

Figure 3-12 illustrates the tiled All Window display on my Mac after I press F3. Move the cursor on top of the window you want to activate — the window border turns blue when it's selected — and then click once to switch to that window. You can specify which keys you want to use within the Mission Control pane in System Preferences.

» Press F10 to show all open, visible windows from the application that you're *currently* using; then click the one that you want to activate. This Mission Control function is great for choosing among all the images that you've opened in Adobe Photoshop or all the Safari web pages littering your Desktop!

An astute observer would notice, in addition to the window switch, that the application menu bar changes to match the now-active application.

» Press F11, and all open windows scurry to the side of the screen (much like a herd of zebras do if you drop a lioness in their midst). Now you can work with drives, files, and aliases on the Desktop — and when you're ready to confront those dozen application windows again, just press the keyboard shortcut a second time.

Scroll Windows

Often, more stuff is in a document or more files are on your hard drive than you can see in the space available for a window. I guess that means it's time to delete stuff. No, no — *just joking!* You don't have to take such drastic measures to see more information in a window.

Just use the scroll bars that you see in **Figure 3-13** to move through the contents of the window. By default, El Capitan displays scroll bars only if they're required. You move your pointer to the side or bottom of the window, but you can control when scroll bars appear in the General pane within System Preferences.

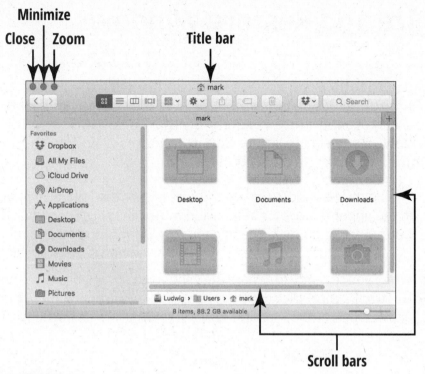

FIGURE 3-13

You can generally scroll in one of two ways:

» **Click the scroll bar and drag it.** For the uninitiated, that means clicking the bar and holding down the mouse button while you move the mouse in the direction you want.

» **Click in the empty area above or below the bar.** This maneuver scrolls pages one at a time.

Depending on the type of application you're using, you might be able to scroll a window with the arrow keys on your keyboard as well — or perhaps press the Page Up and Page Down keys to move in a window. Today's Magic Mouse 2 and Magic Trackpad 2 also allow scrolling by using gestures.

Minimize and Restore Windows

The multitalented Figure 3-13, shown in the preceding section, displays another control that you can use with a window: the Minimize button. When you *minimize* a window, you eliminate it from the Desktop and store it safely on the Dock. After you minimize a window, you need to know how to restore it. Follow these steps to minimize and restore a window:

1. To minimize a window, move the cursor over the Minimize button in the upper-left corner of the window (a minus sign appears on the button) and then click. The minimized window appears as a miniature icon on the Dock so that you can keep an eye on it, so to speak.

2. When you're ready to *restore* the window (display it again on the Desktop), simply click the thumbnail icon representing the window on the Dock, and OS X automagically returns it to its former size and location.

Zoom Windows

Zooming windows has kind of a Flash Gordon sound to it, don't you think? It's nothing quite that exciting — no red tights or laser guns. Still, when you're trying to view a larger portion of a document, *zooming* is a good thing because it expands the window to the maximum practical size for the application you're using (and the content being displayed). When you want to zoom, here's what you need to know:

» **You can zoom with one click.** To zoom a window, move the cursor over the Zoom/Full Screen button in the upper-left corner of the window. Figure 3-13, shown earlier in this chapter, struts its stuff (again) and illustrates the position. (That is one versatile figure!) When you hold down the Option key, a plus sign appears on the Zoom/Full Screen button. While holding down the Option key, click to expand your horizons.

TIP

When you finish with a zoomed window, you can return it to its previous dimensions by clicking the Zoom/Full Screen button again.

» **Zooming produces mixed results.** In some cases, zooming a window fills the entire screen; at other times, the extra space would be wasted, so the application zooms the window to the maximum size that shows as much content as possible (with no unnecessary white space).

» **You can't zoom in on everything.** The Zoom button can even be disabled by an application that doesn't want you to muck about with the window. I own a game or two that doesn't allow zooming, for example.

"But Mark, what happens when I *don't* hold down the Option key?" A great question! If you move your cursor over the Zoom/Full Screen button, you'll notice that it carries a pair of opposing arrows. Click the button to switch to El Capitan's Full Screen mode, in which the window occupies the entire screen. (To return the application to windowed mode, press Esc.)

Move and Resize Windows

Finder and application windows on your Mac Desktop are unlike the (rather) permanent windows in your home; you can pick a window and cart it to another portion of the Desktop. Here are the basics of moving windows:

» **Move windows when you want to see other stuff.** Typically, you move a window when you're using more than one application at a time and need to see the contents of multiple windows.

» **Click and drag the window to move it.** To grab a window and make off with it, click the window's *title bar* — the strip at the top of the window that usually bears a document or application name — and drag the window to the new location. Then release the mouse button to plant it firmly in the new location.

» **Change the width or height of the window instead.** To change the dimensions of a window to your exact specifications, move the pointer over any edge of the window, click, and then drag until the window is the size you prefer.

Close Windows

When you're finished with a document or you no longer need a window open, you can close it to free that space on the Desktop. As with most tasks on the Mac, closing windows is simple:

» **Close a window with the Close button.** Move the cursor over the Close button; it's the circular button in the upper-left corner of the window (refer to Figure 3-11). An X appears on the button when you're in the zone. When the X appears, just click. Most programs also have Close commands on their File menus.

» **Save your information if you're asked to save before closing.** Most Mac applications don't want you closing a window willy-nilly if you change the contents without saving them. Try to close a document window in Microsoft Word or Pages (see Chapter 8) without saving the file first. The program asks for confirmation before it closes the window containing your unsaved Great American Novel. (Here's another indicator: Some programs display a black dot in the center of the program's Close button to indicate unsaved changes.)

To close all windows displayed by a particular program, hold down the Option key while you click the Close button in one of the windows. Whoosh! They're all gone.

Close Programs

If I had a twisted and warped sense of humor, I would tell you to close applications simply by pulling the Mac power cord from the wall socket. (Luckily, I don't.) You have saner ways to close a program, however. Use one of these methods instead:

» Press the ⌘+Q keyboard shortcut.

» Choose the application's named menu (for example, Pages or Word or iTunes) and then click Quit.

» Right-click the application icon on the Dock and choose Quit from the menu that appears.

You can also click the Close button in the application window. Note, however, that this technique doesn't always close the application.

TIP

You may be able to close a program's window without closing the program itself. You can close a browser window in Safari, for example, but the Safari program continues to run. When you close a program completely, you automatically close any windows that the program opened.

Chapter 4
Customizing El Capitan

El Capitan is easy to customize in many ways: You can adjust the appearance of the Desktop, configure the behavior of your mouse (or trackpad) and keyboard, and set up a screen saver to keep your Mac happy while you're away.

In this chapter, I show you how to

» Select a background, an appearance, and icon arrangement for the Desktop.

» Tweak the behavior of your pointing device and keyboard.

» Enhance the readability of the Desktop.

» Use the El Capitan visual cues rather than system sounds.

» Enable dictation.

Fine-Tune El Capitan

Your Mac is truly easy to customize to your specific desires and needs. Because each user on your Mac has individual Desktop settings, you can quickly make changes to *your* Desktop configuration *without* upsetting the other members of the family (who may not want a hot-pink background with lime-green highlights).

 Most changes you make to customize your Mac require you to open the System Preferences window, which you can reach by clicking the System Preferences icon on the Dock. (The icon bears a number of gears for a label.)

Change the Desktop Background

I have yet to meet a computer owner who didn't change the Desktop background when presented with the opportunity. Favorite backgrounds usually include

» Humorous cartoons and photos

» Scenic beauty

» Simple solid colors that help icons and windows stand out

» Photos of family and friends

If you decide to spruce up your background, you have three choices: Select one of the default OS X background images, choose a solid color, or specify your own image. All three background types are available from the Desktop & Screen Saver pane, located within System Preferences, as shown in **Figure 4-1**.

 If you haven't enabled right-clicking on your mouse or trackpad yet — Apple calls it this a *secondary click* — I recommend doing so now. Open System Preferences, click the Mouse (or Trackpad) icon, and then select Point & Click tab. Click the Secondary Click check box to enable it. Now you can right-click by tapping the

TIP

mouse at the right corner (or right-click the trackpad with two fingers). You can right-click any open spot on the Desktop and choose Change Desktop Background from the pop-up shortcut menu, for example.

The well

Select a background image.

FIGURE 4-1

To choose a background from one of the collections provided by Apple, click one of these groups in the list on the left:

>> **Desktop Pictures:** These backgrounds feature scenic beauty, such as blades of grass, sand dunes, snowy hills . . . that sort of thing. You also get close-up backgrounds of plant life — I especially recommend the green grass — and several truly beautiful portraits of Yosemite and El Capitan.

>> **Solid Colors:** This collection is for those who desire a soothing solid shade.

» **Photos:** Choose an image from your Photos Library. (Note that the iPhoto and Aperture groups appear only if you've installed those applications.)

» **Pictures:** This option displays the images saved in your Pictures folder.

» **Choose Folder:** You can open a folder containing images and display them instead. (I discuss this in more detail in a page or two.)

If you see something you like, click the thumbnail, and OS X automatically refreshes the background so that you can see what it looks like. (There's no OK, Accept, or Apply button to click.)

You'll note that OS X provides five orientations for your background image. First, click the pop-up menu next to the preview image in the top-left corner of the pane (refer to Figure 4-1). Then you can choose to

» **Tile the background.** The image is repeated to cover the Desktop (usually done with pattern images to produce a smooth look).

» **Fill the screen.** The original aspect ratio of the image is preserved, so it's not stretched.

» **Fit to screen.** Choose this option to resize the height or width of the image to fit your screen, keeping the original aspect ratio.

» **Stretch the background to fill the Desktop.** If your Desktop image is smaller than the Desktop acreage, be warned: If you try to stretch too small an image over too large a Desktop, the pixilated result can be frightening. (Think of enlarging an old Kodak Instamatic negative to a 16 × 20 poster. Dots, dots, dots.) Also, the original aspect ratio of the image isn't preserved, so you may end up with stretched results that look like a funhouse mirror at a carnival.

» **Center the image on the Desktop.** This solution is my favorite for Desktop images that are smaller than the screen resolution.

This pop-up menu appears only if the Desktop picture you select isn't one of the standard Apple images. All pictures in the Desktop Pictures and Solid Colors categories are scaled automatically to the size of your screen.

To change the Desktop background automatically from the selected folder, select the Change Picture check box and then choose the delay period from the corresponding pop-up menu (refer to Figure 4-1). To display the images within the selected folder in random order, also select the Random Order check box; otherwise, OS X displays the images in the order in which they appear in the folder.

As I mention earlier in this chapter, if you want your favorite color without the distraction of an image, you can choose among a selection of solid colors. You can choose these colors the same way that you pick a default OS X background image, as I describe earlier in this section.

Finally, you can drag your own image into the well from a Finder window to add your own work of art. To view the thumbnails from an entire folder, click the Pictures folder (to display the contents of your personal Pictures folder) or click the Add button (bearing the plus sign) to specify any folder on your system. Click one of the thumbnails (the small images) to embellish the Desktop.

You can also set a screen saver from this dialog. Flip ahead to the section "Select a Screen Saver" for more information.

Change the Desktop Color Scheme

You can select your own colors for buttons, menus, and windows within El Capitan, and just like your background choice, the color scheme you select is completely up to you. (Some color schemes supplied by Apple may also help with any reduced vision you may have.) To choose a scheme, follow these steps:

1. Open System Preferences and click the General icon to display the settings shown in **Figure 4-2**.

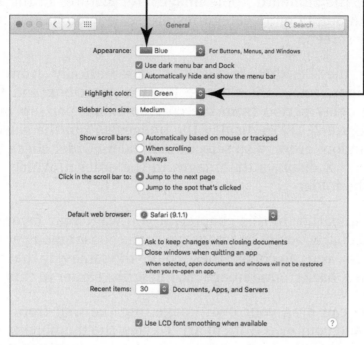

Choose the main color for buttons and menus.

Choose the color that appears when you select text or other items.

FIGURE 4-2

2. Click the Appearance pop-up menu, and choose the main color choice for your buttons, windows, and menus (either Blue or Graphite).

3. Click the Highlight Color pop-up menu, and pick the highlight color that appears when you select text in an application or select an item from a list.

4. Press ⌘+Q to close System Preferences and save your changes.

Select a Screen Saver

Screen savers are also popular customizable display items. True, today's LED monitors don't require animated graphics to avoid burn-in, the way that older CRT tube-based monitors did, but the moving colors and images displayed by a screen saver can still provide security as well as a bit of fun to your desktop. A screen saver runs after the specified amount of inactivity has passed.

To select a screen saver, open System Preferences and click the Desktop & Screen Saver icon; then click the Screen Saver tab to display the settings you see in **Figure 4-3**. Click the Start After pop-up menu to control the inactivity delay (or choose Never to disable the screen-saver feature).

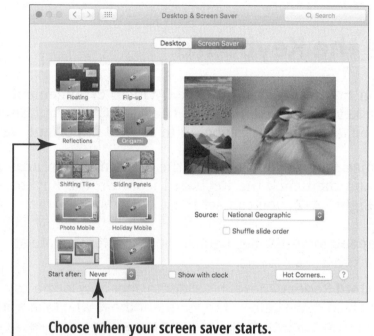

Choose when your screen saver starts.

Select a screen saver.

FIGURE 4-3

Click one of the entries in the Screen Savers column to display a thumb-nail showing the effect. Selecting the Random thumbnail, naturally, runs through them all. You can also test the appearance of the saver module by clicking the Preview button; the screen saver runs until you move the mouse, move your finger across the trackpad, or press a key.

Many screen savers let you monkey with their settings. If the Options button is enabled (not grayed out), click it to see how you can change the effects.

TIP

Click the Hot Corners button to display the Hot Corner sheet. There, you can click any of the four pop-up menus in the four corners of the screen display to specify that corner as an *activation hot corner* (which immediately activates the screen saver) or as a *disabling hot corner* (which prevents the screen saver from being activated). As long as the cursor stays in the disabling hot corner, the screen saver doesn't kick in, no matter how long a period of inactivity passes. Click OK to save your changes and return to the System Preferences window.

Customize the Keyboard

No, you can't rearrange that horrible QWERTY arrangement by pulling off the keys — believe me, I've tried — but El Capitan lets you tweak the behavior of your keyboard in several important ways.

To customize your keyboard, click the System Preferences icon on the Dock and then click the Keyboard icon. On the Keyboard pane, shown in **Figure 4-4**, you can set these options:

» **Key Repeat:** Move the Key Repeat slider to alter the rate at which a keystroke repeats.

» **Delay Until Repeat:** Move this slider to alter how long a key must be held down before it repeats. For those who take a little more time pressing each key, moving this slider to the left helps reduce unwanted repeats.

El Capitan also provides the Sticky Keys and Slow Keys features, which can help you if you have trouble pressing keyboard shortcuts or if you often trigger keyboard repeats (repetition of the same character) accidentally. To use these options, display the System Preferences window, click the Accessibility icon, and then click the Keyboard icon in the list on the left.

Sticky Keys work by allowing you to press the modifier keys in a key sequence (such as ⌘+A) one after another rather than all at the same time. Slow Keys allows a pause between the moment a key is pressed and the moment that El Capitan acts on the keystroke. To turn on either feature (or both), just select the corresponding Enable check box.

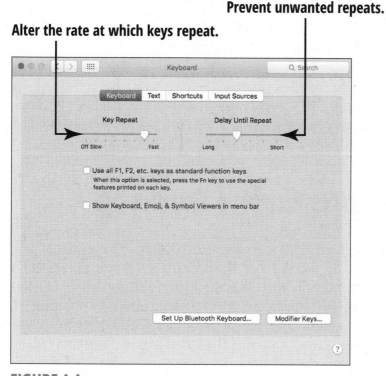

FIGURE 4-4

You can modify the way that Sticky Keys work by clicking the corresponding Options button and selecting these settings:

» **Press the Shift Key Five Times:** Select this check box and then you can toggle Sticky Keys on and off from the keyboard by pressing the Shift key five times.

» **Beep When a Modifier Key Is Set:** Select this check box to play a beep when El Capitan recognizes that you've activated a modifier key.

» **Display Pressed Keys on Screen:** Select this check box, and El Capitan displays each key you press in a Sticky Keys sequence to help you keep track of the characters you've entered.

You can modify the way that Slow Keys work by clicking the corresponding Options button and using these settings:

» **Use Click Key Sounds:** Select this check box to add a key-click sound every time you press a key.

» **Acceptance Delay:** Drag this slider to specify the length of the delay before the key is accepted.

To turn off keyboard repeat — which may be required, depending on the settings you choose for Sticky Keys and Slow Keys — click the Open Keyboard Preferences button, which displays the Keyboard preference settings I discuss earlier in this chapter.

Organize Icons on the Desktop

Consider the layout of the Desktop itself. You can set the options for your Desktop icons from the Finder's View menu (click any open part of the Desktop and choose View➪Show View Options) or by right-clicking any open part of the Desktop and choosing Show View Options. (Heck, you can even press ⌘+J.) Whichever route you choose, El Capitan displays the dialog that you see in **Figure 4-5**.

The changes you can make from this dialog include

» **Resize icons.** Click and drag the Icon Size slider to shrink or expand the icons on the Desktop. The icon size is displayed in pixels above the slider.

» **Specify grid spacing.** Click and drag the Grid Spacing slider to shrink or expand the grid used to align icons on the Desktop. The larger the grid, the more space between icons.

» **Resize icon label text.** Click the up and down arrows to the right of the Text Size pop-up menu to choose the font size (in points) for icon labels.

Change the size of your icons.

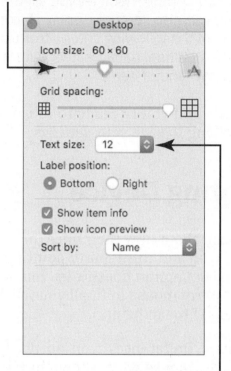

Change the size of the icon labels.

FIGURE 4-5

» **Move icon label text.** Select the Bottom (default) or Right radio button to choose between displaying the text under or to the right of your Desktop icons.

» **Show item info.** With the Show Item Info check box selected, OS X displays the number of items within each folder on the Desktop, as well as the size and free space on your hard drives.

» **Show icon preview.** Select the Show Icon Preview check box, and the Finder displays icons for image files, using a miniature of the original picture. (It's a cool feature for people with digital cameras, but it takes extra processing time because OS X has to load each image file and shrink it to create the icon.)

>> **Sort.** The options in the Sort By pop-up menu let you align icons to a grid on the Desktop. You can also sort the display of icons in a window by choosing one of the following criteria from its pop-up menu: by name, date modified, date created, date last opened, date added, size, or the kind of item.

After all your changes are made and you're ready to return to work, click the Close button of the dialog to save your settings.

Customize Your Pointing Device

Mac owners are downright picky about how their mice (or trackpads) work, and that includes folks who add third-party pointing devices, such as trackballs. Once again, El Capitan doesn't let you down, and you can customize your third-party mouse to fit all your clicking and double-clicking quirks (whoops, I mean habits).

To get started, click the System Preferences icon on the Dock and then click the Mouse icon. On the Mouse pane, shown in **Figure 4-6**, you find these settings:

>> **Tracking Speed:** Drag this slider to determine how fast the mouse tracks across the Desktop.

>> **Double-Click Speed:** Drag the Double-Click Speed slider to determine how fast you must click your mouse to cause a double-click.

>> **Scrolling Speed:** Drag this slider to specify the rate at which the contents of windows will scroll.

>> **Primary Mouse Button:** For those lefties who want to change the primary mouse button, select the Right radio button to switch to the right button as your primary button.

>> **Scroll Direction:** If your mouse has a scroll wheel or ball, you can specify whether the contents of a window should move up or down when you scroll.

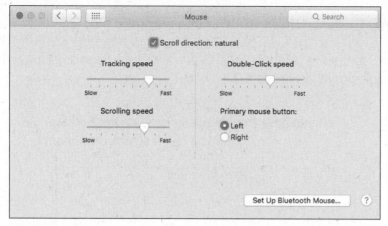

FIGURE 4-6

If you're using a MacBook laptop — or a desktop Mac and a Magic Trackpad 2 — you'll find many of these same settings on the System Preferences Trackpad pane. You can also choose which gestures your Mac will recognize, such as tap-to-click, zooming, and swiping between pages. The Trackpad pane includes a short video demonstrating each gesture, and you can modify many of the gestures by specifying the number of fingers to use and the sequence of taps that will trigger the action.

Set Your Screen for Maximum Visibility

Two features in El Capitan can help people with limited vision: First, you can change the display resolution and brightness so that onscreen elements are easier to distinguish. Second, you can use the Accessibility Display tools to enhance the clarity of your Desktop, Finder windows, and program windows.

Your monitor can display different resolutions, and the higher the resolution, the smaller that items appear onscreen. So if you want items on the Desktop to appear larger, you have to lower the screen resolution. You can also change the brightness level of your display to match the ambient lighting in the room.

To change these settings, follow these steps:

1. Open System Preferences, and click the Display icon to display the settings shown in **Figure 4-7**.

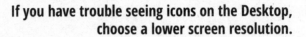

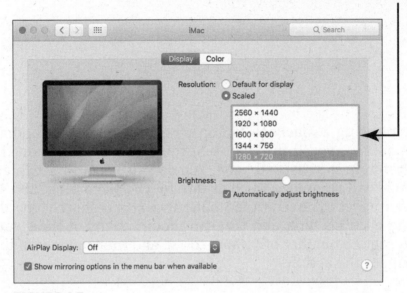

FIGURE 4-7

2. Click the Scaled radio button; then click the resolution you want to use in the list that appears.

If you're having problems discerning items on the Desktop, try a lower resolution.

TIP

3. (Optional) By default, El Capitan sets the brightness of your screen automatically based on the ambient lighting around your Mac. If you'd like to specify a brightness level yourself, click the Automatically Adjust Brightness check box and drag the Brightness slider to the desired level.

4. Press ⌘+Q to close System Preferences and save your changes.

Use the Accessibility Tools

El Capitan offers advanced features (grouped under the name Accessibility) that can help with contrast and zooming for Mac owners with limited vision.

To turn on the Accessibility options, follow these steps:

1. Open System Preferences, click the Accessibility icon, and then click the Zoom entry on the left to see the settings shown in **Figure 4-8**.

Click to set zoom options.

Click to enable display zoom using keyboard.

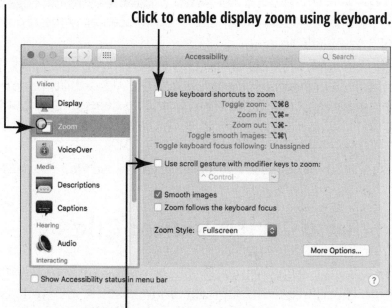

Click to enable display zoom using gestures.

FIGURE 4-8

2. To turn on El Capitan's Zoom feature for your display — which allows you to zoom in on a selected portion of the screen — click the Use Keyboard Shortcuts to Zoom check box. (Alternatively, you can scroll using your pointing device while holding down the specified modifier key.)

3. To specify how much magnification is used, click the More Options button. On the sheet that appears, you can set the minimum and maximum Zoom magnification increments. From the keyboard, press ⌘+Option+= (equal sign) to zoom in or press ⌘+Option+– (minus sign) to zoom out. You can also display a preview rectangle of the area that's included when you zoom.

To have OS X smooth images to make them look better when zoomed, select the Smooth Images check box.

TIP

If you click the More Options button, you can also determine how the screen moves in relation to the pointer from the Zoom Options sheet: By default, the zoomed screen moves with the pointer, but you can set it to move only when the pointer reaches the edge of the screen or maintain the pointer near the center of the zoomed image automatically.

4. (Optional) If you prefer white text on a black background, click the Display icon in the list on the left side of the Accessibility pane and select the Invert Colors check box. Note that depending on your display settings, it may be easier on the eyes to use Grayscale Display mode by selecting the Use Grayscale check box.

5. Press ⌘+Q to close System Preferences and save your changes.

Replace Sounds with Visual Cues

El Capitan can provide additional visual cues to supplement the spoken and audio alerts used throughout your system, as well as convert stereo audio to mono (useful for folks with diminished hearing in one ear).

Follow these steps to use these features:

1. Open System Preferences, click the Accessibility icon, and then click the Audio icon to display the options shown in **Figure 4-9**.

2. Select the Flash the Screen When an Alert Sound Occurs check box, and click the Test Screen Flash button to test the visual cues.

Make the screen flash when an audio alert sounds.

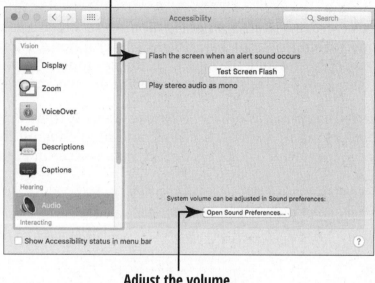

Adjust the volume.

FIGURE 4-9

3. To play stereo music as mono (with both channels combined as one channel from both speakers), click the Play Stereo Audio As Mono check box to select it.

TIP

To raise the overall sound volume in OS X, click the Open Sound Preferences button to display the Sound settings, where you can drag the Volume slider to the right.

Set Up Dictation

Since the early days of the Mac OS, Apple has included some form of speech functionality in its computers. El Capitan continues to improve on speech recognition by offering a host of tools that let you get more work done in a shorter amount of time.

The dictation feature within OS X let you speak to your Mac directly, providing text entry in all sorts of applications. (My favorites are Pages, Messages, and Mail.) Luckily, you probably won't need to buy any fancy extra equipment to use dictation. Most current Mac models have a built-in microphone. If you use an iMac, your microphone is built into the monitor, and MacBooks have a similar microphone built into the screen. (Even many Mac monitors include a camera and microphone.) If your Mac doesn't have a microphone, though, find yourself a simple one and connect it to the computer by plugging it into the Line-In or Microphone jack, which I discuss in Chapter 2.

To get started with dictation in OS X, open the System Preferences window by clicking its icon on the Dock and then clicking the Dictation & Speech icon, which displays the settings you see in **Figure 4-10**.

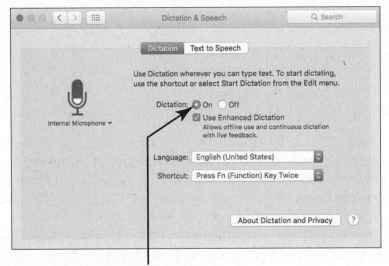

Turn on speech recognition.

FIGURE 4-10

The Dictation & Speech pane consists of two tabs:

» **Dictation:** The Dictation tab provides settings that control how your Mac listens to Its Master's Voice. (That means you, friend reader.) You can set the sound input and adjust the key on the keyboard that toggles Dictation on and off. To enable dictation, click the Dictation On radio button. Now you can set your cursor within any application that accepts typed characters, press the dictation shortcut key, and begin speaking! El Capitan displays a pop-up Dictation menu that appears next to the application window, complete with a sound-level indicator. To stop dictating, click the Done button on the Dictation pop-up menu.

TIP

Click the Sound Input icon to select the device that will be used for dictation. (If your Mac has a built-in microphone, El Capitan will use Internal Microphone by default.) If you've added a USB or Line-In microphone, you can choose it here.

TIP

By default, the dictation feature requires you to be connected to the Internet. If you click the Use Enhanced Dictation check box, however, El Capitan downloads an additional file that allows dictation even when you're not connected. I recommend it!

» **Text to Speech:** Did I also mention that your Mac can actually read text to you? Click this tab to choose a systemwide voice, announce alerts out loud, and speak selected text when you press a specified key. You can also jump to the Date & Time Preferences pane and set El Capitan to announce the time.

Chapter 5

Working with Files and Folders

O S X is a highly visual operating system, and using it without a pointing device (like a mouse or trackpad) is like building Hoover Dam with a pocketknife (and not a particularly sharp pocketknife, either). Therefore, most of this chapter requires you to firmly grasp the little rodent or place your finger squarely on your trackpad. I introduce you to items such as *files* and *folders* and lead you through the basic training you need to run programs and open documents.

I also show you just how easy it is to manage your files and folders as gracefully as Fred Astaire on his best day. You'll also see how to keep your Mac tidy and organized so that you can find things more easily and work more efficiently:

>> Create, select, and open files and folders.

>> Copy and move files and folders.

>> View documents and launch your favorite applications with a single click or press of a key.

Store Files on Your Mac

Although you may already be familiar with how your information is stored in files, I want to cover the big concepts you need to know about files, just in case:

>> **The information you use and the stuff you create are saved in files.** A *file* is an individual item that has its own name and properties, such as the date it was created and which program runs it. A letter you write, a photo you take, and your genealogical data you cataloged are all stored in individual files.

>> **You run programs to create and edit files.** A *program* is used to do work on a computer (such as Pages, which you would use to type that letter). In the Mac world, a program is often referred to as an *application* (or *app*). So a program and an application are exactly the same thing!

>> **Files are linked to programs.** Here's one of the features that makes the Mac so neat! Double-click a Pages document you created (again, that same doggone letter I keep mentioning), and

El Capitan automatically knows that the Pages program has to run for you to work with that document — say, make changes in the letter or print it. Then the needed program automatically launches and loads the letter file, ready for you to use. The file is marked as a Pages document, and El Capitan maintains the link between them. *Snazzy!*

TIP

Although each file is individually named, El Capitan tries to make it as easy as possible to visually identify which program owns which file. Therefore, most programs use a special icon to indicate their data files. **Figure 5-1** illustrates several document and data files created by a range of programs: each of the four columns of icons represent files from Photos, Pages, Automator, and Safari (from left to right).

» **Word processing and desktop publishing files are called documents.** A *document* is just a special kind of file. Both a newsletter created in Pages and a home budget spreadsheet created in Numbers are documents.

Documents and files

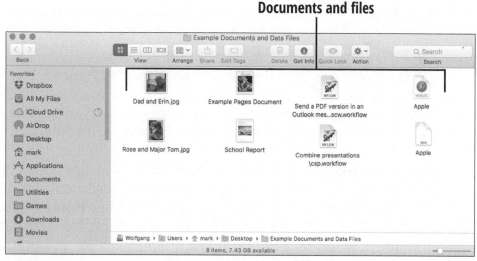

FIGURE 5-1

Organize Files with Folders

"Mark, I thought this computer was going to get me away from all that paper in my filing cabinets!" Don't worry, dear reader: Your Mac can indeed create a paper-free zone in your home office. Start off by thinking of your Mac as a big filing cabinet.

» A *folder* is simply a container that you can use to hold one or more files on your Mac, just like an actual manila folder that (ideally) gets put away neatly in a cabinet drawer. (The folks who designed the first Mac operating system decades ago knew that we're all comfortable with the idea of storing information in folders, so they used the idea.)

» You can organize your files on the Desktop and within Finder windows by copying and moving files in and out of folders (or, in brave moments, even between folders). (Chapter 8 explains how to cut, copy, and paste.) This process is no different from moving a piece of paper from a manila folder to another.

» Folders can be named, renamed, and deleted, just as files can. (Sections later in this chapter explain how.) You can also create a folder within a folder to further organize your stuff, and these "enclosed" folders are *subfolders*.

» As you can see from the assortment shown in **Figure 5-2**, folders have a 3-D look in OS X. In fact, major system folders (including Applications, Downloads, Library, System, Users, and Utilities) sport folder icons in El Capitan that identify their contents.

Every user account that you create on your Mac has a special folder, called a Home folder, where you can store documents and data for your use. No one else can see the contents of your Home folder, which is named after your account. (Visiting your Home folder is easy. Open any Finder window, and you'll see it below the Favorites heading in the sidebar at the left side of the window.)

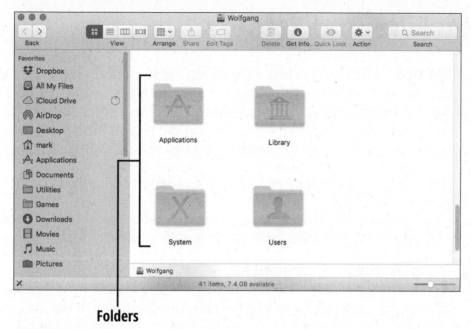

Folders

FIGURE 5-2

Inside your Home folder are subfolders that are automatically created as well, and you can use these folders to store all sorts of documents and help keep your Mac organized. The most important Home sub-folders include

» **Documents:** This subfolder is provided so that you can store all sorts of documents you've created, such as your Pages projects. El Capitan also places a link to your Documents folder on the Dock.

» **Downloads:** You'll also find this subfolder on the Dock. By default, Safari stores all files you've downloaded from the web in this subfolder.

» **Movies, Music, and Pictures:** These three subfolders are self-explanatory. They store any movies, digital music files (including your iTunes music library), and photos that you upload from your camera or snap with your FaceTime camera.

Open Files and Folders

To open a folder within El Capitan, just double-click it. (Alternatively, you can click it to select it and then press ⌘+O.) The contents of the folder — documents, photo files, and so on — are displayed within a new window or within the current window (depending on how you set View mode, which you can read about in Chapter 3).

Here's the simple way to load a document:

1. If a Finder window isn't already open, double-click your Mac's hard-drive icon on the Desktop. This step opens a Finder window.

   TIP

   See Chapter 3 if you need a little help finding this icon on your Desktop.

2. Double-click the folder that contains the document. If the document is stored in a subfolder, double-click that subfolder to open it.

3. When the document is visible, double-click it. (This method is my preferred method because I'm an ALT — short for *Admittedly Lazy Technowizard* — who would rather use complex hand movements to pour myself another Diet Coke.)

If the program that you created the document with is already open, you can also open a document from inside the program. I already have Pages open, for example, I can open a Pages document from there.

Follow these steps to open a document from within an application:

1. Choose File ➪ Open or press the handy ⌘+O key combination. Your OS X application is likely to display the attractive Open dialog that you see in **Figure 5-3**. Note that you can switch the Open dialog between view modes (see Chapter 3), just like you can switch view modes within a Finder window, so you can browse in Icon mode, List mode or Column mode. (For this demonstration, I use Column mode, which is my favorite view mode.)

View icons

Pop-up menu

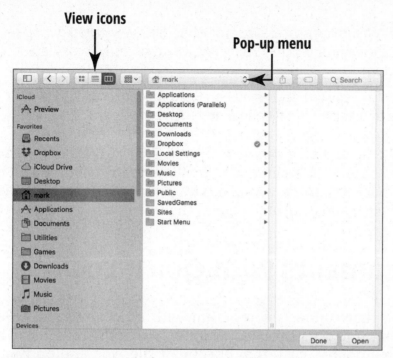

FIGURE 5-3

2. Navigate to the location of the document you want to open. In the Open dialog, you can navigate in one of two ways:

- Use the pop-up menu at the top center of the dialog or the sidebar at the left to jump directly to common locations — such as the Desktop, your iCloud Drive, and your Home folder, as well as places you recently accessed (Recent Places).

- If the target folder isn't on your pop-up menu, move the slider near the bottom of the dialog to the far left to display your hard drives, DVD drives, and network locations.

    If you're having trouble locating the file or enclosing folder, click the Search box in the upper-right corner of the Open dialog and type the first few letters of the name to display files with matching names on your Mac.

TIP

3. Click the location where the file is stored (usually within at least one folder). Note that the right columns change to show you the contents of the item you just clicked. In this way, you can cruise through successive folders to find that elusive document. (This somewhat

time-consuming process is somewhat derisively called *drilling* — hence the importance of using Recent Items, as I discuss later in this chapter.)

4. When you spy the document you want to load, double-click it, or click once to highlight the filename and then click Open.

TIP

"Hey, the Open dialog can be resized!" That's right, good reader. You can expand the Open dialog to show more columns and find things more easily. As you can with any window in El Capitan, you can click and drag any edge of the Open dialog to resize it.

View Documents with Quick Look

The link that connects a program with a document is A Beautiful Thing, but sometimes you just want to look at the contents of a file — and if you double-click that document file, you end up waiting for the entire application to load. (Depending on the size of the program, this process can take as long as 10 or 15 seconds!) There has to be an easier way to just take a gander at what's inside a document, right?

Don't think that I would have gone that far into a fancy introduction if the answer were negative. I'm ushering in the El Capitan Quick Look feature, which can display the contents of many documents — but without *opening* the corresponding program! This capability is one reason why you bought a Mac.

To use Quick Look from a Finder window, follow these steps:

1. Click to select a file.

2. Press the spacebar. **Figure 5-4** illustrates Quick Look in action, this time displaying the contents of a Pages document.

TIP

As with other windows in El Capitan, you can click the lower-right corner of the Quick Look window and drag it to resize the window. To display the Quick Look window full-screen, click the double-arrow button at the top-left corner of the window. Press Esc to banish the window and return to your desktop.

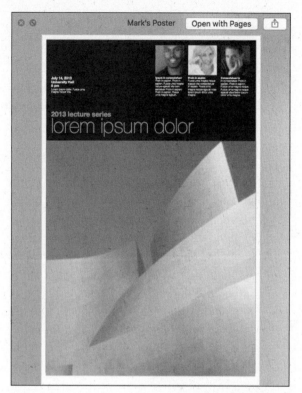

FIGURE 5-4

3. Press Esc (or click the Close button in the upper-left corner of the Quick Look window) when you're done checking out the document.

View Images and PDF Documents with Preview

Along with Quick Look, El Capitan offers a Swiss Army Knife application for viewing image files and PDF documents: namely, Preview. You can use Preview to display virtually all popular types of digital photos produced by today's cameras (and available for downloading on the web).

If you haven't heard of *PDF* documents, think of a printed document in electronic format. You can view PDF documents on your screen, but typically, you can't modify them. (Many publishers sell e-books in PDF format because PDF documents can be viewed on just about any computer or tablet available these days; virtually all smartphones can display them as well.)

El Capitan automatically loads Preview when you double-click an image in a format it recognizes or when you double-click a PDF file. Check out the image displayed in Preview in **Figure 5-5**, which shows the toolbar. It also acts as a Print Preview window. If you want to launch Preview manually, click the Launchpad icon on the Dock and then click the Preview icon. (Read all about Launchpad in Chapter 3.)

Preview toolbar

FIGURE 5-5

I know — if that were the sum total of Preview's features, Preview wouldn't deserve coverage here. What else can it do? Here's a partial list (just my favorites, mind you):

» Start a full-screen slideshow of the pages in a PDF document by choosing View ⇨ Slideshow. Press the Esc key to return to the Preview window.

» Add a bookmark to a specific page in a PDF document by choosing Tools ⇨ Add Bookmark. You can display bookmarked pages by choosing View ⇨ Bookmarks.

» Take a *screen snapshot* (save the contents of your screen as a digital photo) by choosing File ⇨ Take Screen Shot ⇨ From Entire Screen. (OS X also includes a screen snapshot capture application called Grab, which you can find in your Applications folder.)

TIP

Taking a snapshot of your screen is a great help when El Capitan displays one of those pesky error messages. Rather than write down cryptic codes and messages, you can show the snapshot to a technician or Mac-savvy friend later!

Create an Alias to a File or Folder

An *alias* acts as a link to another item elsewhere on your system. To load an Adobe Acrobat document (otherwise called a PDF), you can click an alias file icon that you can create on the Desktop (or add to your Dock) rather than click the actual file icon itself. The alias acts essentially the same way as the original icon, but it doesn't occupy the same space — only a few bytes for the icon itself compared with the size of the actual file. In addition, you don't have to dig through folders galore to find the original document.

TIP

You can always identify an alias by the small curved arrow at the base of the icon. The icon may also sport the tag alias at the end of its name.

You have two ways to create an alias. You can

1. Select the item.

2. Choose File ➪ Make Alias or press ⌘+L.

Here's another way to create an alias:

1. Press and hold the key combination ⌘+Option.

2. Drag the original icon to the location where you want the alias.

Note that this method doesn't add the `alias` tag to the end of the alias icon name, but you *can* see the tiny curved arrow as you drag the icon.

Why bother to use an alias? Here are two good reasons:

» **Open a document from anywhere on your drive.** You can open a Numbers spreadsheet from the Desktop, for example, by using an alias that you created there, no matter where the actual document file resides. Speed, organization, and convenience — life is good.

» **Send an alias to the Trash without affecting the original item.** When that volunteer project is finished, you can safely delete the alias (sending it to the Trash) without worry.

If you move or rename the original file, El Capitan is smart enough to update the alias, too! If the original file is deleted, however, the alias no longer works. Go figure.

Launch Recently Used Documents and Programs

Apple knows that most folks work on the same documents and use the same programs during the course of a day. You might use Photos several times to edit different images, for example, or use Keynote to edit your presentation project many times in the span of a day.

To make it easier to access these frequently used programs and documents, El Capitan includes the Recent Items list. Follow these steps to use it:

1. Click the Apple symbol (🍎) on the menu bar to display the 🍎 menu.

2. Hover the pointer over the Recent Items menu item. The Finder displays all applications and documents you used over the past few computing sessions. If you open a lot of documents and applications, your Recent Items list may cover only your current session.

3. Click an item to load that document or application.

Select Items

Often, the menu commands or keyboard commands you perform in the Finder need to be performed *on* something. Perhaps you're moving an item from one window to another or creating an alias for that item. To identify the target of your action to the Finder, you need to *select* one or more items on your Desktop or in a Finder window. In this section, I show you just how to do that.

El Capitan gives you a couple of options when you're selecting just one item for an upcoming action:

» **Move the pointer over the item and click.** A dark border (or *highlight)* appears around the icon, indicating that it's selected.

» **If an icon is already highlighted on the Desktop or within a window, move the selection highlight to another icon in the same location by using the arrow keys.** To shift the selection highlight alphabetically, press Tab (to move in order) or press Shift+Tab (to move in reverse order).

Selecting items in the Finder doesn't *do* anything to them. You have to *perform an action* on the selected items to make something happen.

TIP

You can also select multiple items with aplomb by using one of these methods:

>> **Adjacent (contiguous) items**

Drag a box around them. If that statement sounds like ancient Sumerian, here's the explanation: Click a spot above and to the left of the first item; then hold down the mouse button (or hold your finger on the trackpad) and drag down and to the right. (This process is called *dragging* in Mac-speak.) An outline such as the one shown in **Figure 5-6** appears, indicating what you're selecting. Any icons that touch or appear within the outline are selected when you release the button.

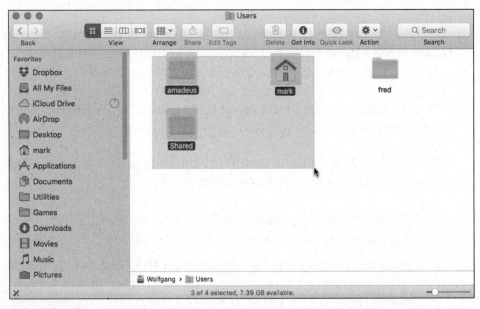

FIGURE 5-6

Click the first item to select it and then hold down the Shift key while you click the last item. El Capitan selects both items and everything between them.

» Nonadjacent items

Select these items by holding down the ⌘ key while you click each item.

Check out the status line at the bottom of a Finder window. It tells how many items are displayed in the current Finder window. When you select items, it shows you how many you highlighted.

Create Folders

In the Mac world, you create new *folders* in a Finder window by using one of these methods:

» With the mouse or trackpad: Right-click in a Finder window or any open space on the Desktop and then choose New Folder from the shortcut menu.

» With the keyboard: Press ⌘+Shift+N.

» From the Finder window toolbar: Click the Action button (which bears a gear icon) and choose New Folder from the menu that appears.

No matter how you create a folder, El Capitan highlights it automatically and places a text cursor below it so that you can immediately type the name for your new folder. Press Return when you're done typing the name.

You'll create folders often to organize documents and files that are related, such as all the images and text you're using for a project.

You can also create *subfolders* inside folders for easier organization. (My tax records, for example, are stored as subfolders named for the tax year, and all of them are located within the Taxes folder on my Desktop.)

Rename Items

You wouldn't go far in today's spacious virtual world without being able to change the moniker of a file or folder. To rename an item in OS X (file or folder), use one of these two methods:

» **The mouse or trackpad:** Click an icon's name just once. Mac OS X highlights the text in an edit box. Type the new name and then press Return when you're done.

» **The Info dialog:** Select the item and press ⌘+I to display the Info dialog; then click the triangle next to Name & Extension. Click the name field, drag the mouse to highlight the text you want to change, and type the replacement text.

The first method is easier, and it's the one I use more often.

TIP

Never rename folders or files in your System directory, and don't rename any of the default subfolders Apple provides in your Home folder. (I discuss these subfolders earlier in this chapter.) Renaming these items may make it harder for you to locate your documents and may even damage your OS X El Capitan installation.

Delete Items You No Longer Need

Even Leonardo da Vinci made the occasional design mistake. I'm guessing that his trash can was likely full of bunched-up pieces of parchment. Luckily, no trees are wasted when you decide to toss your unneeded files and folders. This section shows you how to delete items from your system.

TIP

By the way, as you'll soon witness for yourself, moving items to the Trash doesn't necessarily mean that they're immediately history.

You have a few ways to toss files into the Trash:

» **Drag unruly files against their will.** In OS X, the familiar Mac Trash can appears at the right edge of the Dock; it's that spiffy-looking opaque white can. You can click and drag the items you selected to the Trash and drop them on top of the can icon to delete them. When the Trash contains at least one item, the wire can icon changes to look as though it's full of trash.

» **Delete with menus.** Click the offending file or folder and choose Finder ➪ File ➪ Move to Trash. Or right-click the item to display the shortcut menu and then choose Move to Trash. You can also click the file or folder, click the Action button on the Finder toolbar, and select Move to Trash from the pop-up menu.

» **Delete with the keyboard.** Click the file or folder to select it and then press ⌘+Delete.

Always double-check the Trash contents and make *absolutely* sure that you want to delete them. Remember, you can't retrieve files from the Trash after you empty it. To check the contents of the Trash, right-click the Trash icon on the Dock and choose Open from the shortcut menu. If you find a file or folder in the Trash that you want to restore, drag the item out of the Trash and drop it within the desired Finder window. If you're not sure where to put the restored item, you can always simply drop the item on the Desktop and move it later.

Copy Files and Folders

It's what life is all about, as George Carlin might have said: managing your stuff. On your Mac, that usually means copying and moving files and folders from one drive to another (or from your Mac's internal hard drive to an external drive). In this section, I show you how to copy items from one Finder window to another or from one location (such as a USB flash drive) to another (such as your Desktop). It's *trés* easy.

TIP

When you open a Finder window, you can always see where the files it contains are located. Just check out the Devices list at the left side of the window, and you'll see that one of the devices is highlighted. You're copying stuff *on the same drive* if both locations are on the same device. If, however, one Finder window is displaying items from your internal hard drive and the other is displaying items from a USB flash drive or an external hard drive, you're copying *between drives.*

» **To copy one item to another location on the same drive:** Hold down the Option key (you don't have to select the icon first) and then click and drag the item from its current home to the new location.

TIP

To put a copy of an item within a folder, just drop the item on top of the receiving folder. If you hold the item you're dragging over the destination folder for a second or two, El Capitan opens a new window so that you can see the contents of the target. (This is a *spring-loaded* folder. Really.)

» **To copy multiple items to another location on the same drive:** Select them all first, hold down the Option key, and then drag and drop one of the selected items where you want it. All the items you selected follow the item you drag. (It's rather like lemmings. Nice touch, don't you think?)

TIP

To help indicate your target when you're copying files, El Capitan highlights the location to show you where the items will end up. (This process works whether the target location is a folder or a drive icon.) If the target location is a window, El Capitan adds a highlight to the window border.

» **To copy one or multiple items on a different drive:** Click and drag the icon (or the selected items if you have more than one) from the original window to a window you open on the target drive. (There's no need to hold down the Option key while copying to a different drive.) You can also drag one item (or a selected group of items) and simply drop the items on top of the drive icon on the Desktop. (If you have a document on your hard drive that you need to transfer to a USB flash drive, you would drag the document icon from its current location to the USB drive icon on your desktop. Unlike when you're creating an alias, El Capitan doesn't add anything to the copy's filename.)

TIP

If you try to move or copy something to a location that already has an item with the same name, a dialog prompts you to decide whether to replace the file or to stop the copy or move procedure and leave the existing file alone. Good insurance, indeed.

Move Things from Place to Place

Moving items from one location to another location on the same drive is the easiest action you can take. Just drag the item (or selected items) to the new location. The item disappears from the original spot and reappears in the new spot.

To move items from one drive to another drive, hold down the ⌘ key while you drag the items to the target location.

Why move a file instead of copying it? It's all about what software developers call *version control*. If you've saved a document to the wrong folder, for example, and you simply copy that file to the location where you actually wanted it, you now have two documents with the same name. Which is the current copy? (You'll have to keep track of that.) If you move the document instead, there's still only one version of the document. Also, moving things helps keep your hard drive neat and organized!

Chapter 6

Working with Printers and Scanners

No matter what you use your Mac for, it can produce outstanding documents with today's printers.

You're not limited to a printer, either: Use a scanner or multifunction printer to produce impressive electronic documents in PDF format.

In this chapter, you find out how to

» Install a local USB printer.

» Print a file.

» Remove a printer from your system.

» Produce a PDF electronic document.

» Install a USB scanner.

Add a USB Printer to Your System

 Here's the most common task that you'll probably want to tackle soon after installing OS X: printing documents. Most of us have a Universal Serial Bus (USB) printer, so as long as your printer is supported by OS X, setting it up is as easy as plugging it into one of your Mac's USB ports (shown in the margin). The Big X does the rest of the work, selecting the proper printer software driver. A *driver* is a program that allows OS X El Capitan to recognize and use your printer.

 You may have to install a driver supplied by your printer manufacturer. If the installation of a driver is required, you should find detailed instructions on loading it as part of the manufacturer's setup instructions. Visit the manufacturer's website via your Safari web browser to download the latest driver software (manufacturers make improvements to their drivers to squash bugs and stay current with updates to El Capitan).

TIP

I know that this process *sounds* too good to be true, but I can tell you from my experiences as a consultant and hardware technician that installing a USB printer is really this simple! 'Nuff said.

Unfortunately, if you're adding a Bluetooth or wireless Ethernet printer to your system, setting things up is more complicated than the convenience of USB (and the installation process varies by manufacturer). Therefore, it's important that you follow the manufacturer's setup instructions carefully.

TIP

Print a File

You didn't read this far into this chapter without a burning desire to print something, so in this task, I go over the printing process in detail.

To print from within any application by using the default page characteristics — standard 8½" x 11" paper, portrait mode, no scaling — follow these steps. For these steps, say you have a document open in Pages (which you can read more about in Chapter 8):

1. Choose File from the toolbar and then Print from the File menu.

   OS X displays the simple version of the Print sheet. To display all the fields you see in **Figure 6-1**, click the Show Details button at the bottom of the dialog.

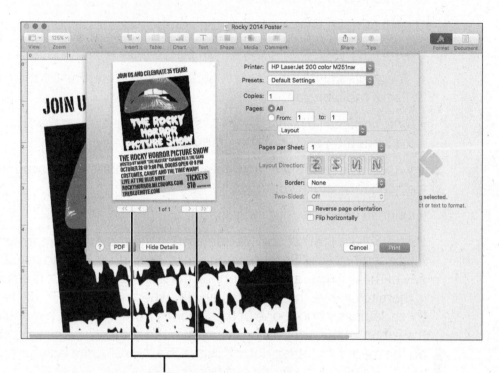

Click these buttons to preview before printing.

FIGURE 6-1

TIP

Some applications (such as Microsoft Word for Mac) use their own custom Print dialogs, but you should see the same general settings as the ones shown in **Figure 6-1**.

TIP

If you want to use a different printer, click the Printer pop-up menu and choose the desired printer. Note that selecting a different printer may automatically change the page characteristics, or you may have to manually select a different page size.

2. Preview your document.

   Would you jump from an airplane without a parachute? Don't waste paper printing a document without double-checking it first. Just click the Page Forward button (the right-arrow icon under the thumbnail image) to check the appearance of each page in your document in the Preview display on the left side of the sheet. If something doesn't look right in the Preview display, click Cancel, and return to your document to fix the problem.

3. Click the Copies field, and enter the number of copies you need.

4. Decide how much of the document you want to print:

   - *The whole shootin' match:* Accept the default All setting for the Pages radio button.

   - *Anything less:* To print a range of selected pages, select the From radio button, and enter the starting and ending pages.

TIP

Try a test print run of the first page before you print a big document. No need to waste ink or toner.

5. (Optional) Choose application-specific printing parameters.

   Each OS X application provides different panes so that you can configure settings specific to that application. You don't have to display any of these extra settings to print a default document, but the power is there to change the look dramatically when necessary. To display these settings, choose one of these panes from the pop-up menu in the center of the Print dialog. (Note that the settings you see depend on the manufacturer's printer driver. A black-and-white laser printer won't display color printing settings, for example.)

6. When everything is go for launch, click the Print button.

Choose a Default Printer

Many Mac owners have more than one printer — perhaps a black-and-white laser printer for plain letters and documents, and an ink-jet printer for projects in which color is important. If you have such a setup, most of your print jobs should be sent to the laser printer (because printing a document with the laser is likely to be cheaper and faster than using the inkjet). The default printer is the one you plan to use for most, if not all, of your print jobs.

You can easily set the default printer within El Capitan! With your default properly set, you don't have to bother choosing a printer on the Print sheet for most jobs; just click Print and go.

To set your default printer, follow these steps:

1. Click the System Preferences icon on the Dock.

2. Click the Printers & Scanners icon to open the Printers & Scanners preferences pane, as shown in **Figure 6-2**.

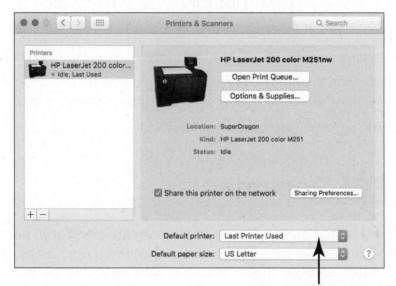

Select a default printer.

FIGURE 6-2

3. Choose one of your installed printers from the Default Printer pop-up menu at the bottom of the pane.

If you choose Last Printer Used, OS X uses the printer that received the last print job.

4. Close the System Preferences window to save the change.

Remove a Printer

If you replace one of your installed printers with a new model, El Capitan can't automatically delete the old printer entry. El Capitan is indeed a very smart operating system, but not *that* smart. Luckily, removing a printer selection from your system is easy:

1. Click the System Preferences icon on the Dock.

2. Click the Printers & Scanners icon to open the Printers & Scanners preferences pane (refer to **Figure 6-2** earlier in this chapter).

3. Click the printer you want to delete.

4. Click the Delete button (carries a minus sign) below the Printers list.

   Depending on the printer manufacturer, you may be prompted for confirmation before the printer entry is removed from the list.

5. Close the System Preferences window to save the change.

Create a PDF Document

The Adobe Acrobat application is used to create electronic documents in PDF format. PDFs are a bit like snapshots of a document, and you typically can't change them, the way you can change a Microsoft Word or a Pages file. However, PDFs can be displayed on virtually all computers and many portable devices (such as mobile phones and tablets), and that's why they're so handy and prevalent on the Internet. Many manufacturers and publishers offer manuals (and books like this) online as PDF files! On a Windows PC, you can use Reader (another program made by Adobe) to read and print PDFs.

Although you certainly can install Adobe Acrobat or Acrobat Reader under El Capitan, I'd be remiss if I didn't mention that you don't *have* to, because OS X provides built-in support for creating, printing, and reading PDFs.

To save a document as a file in PDF format from just about any Mac application, follow these steps:

1. Within your application, open the document you want to save as a PDF, and choose File ➪ Print or press ⌘+P.

   OS X displays the Print sheet (refer to **Figure 6-1** earlier in this chapter).

2. Click the PDF button and then choose Save As PDF from the drop-down menu that appears.

   El Capitan displays the Save sheet, as shown in **Figure 6-3**.

Enter a title.   **Choose a location.**

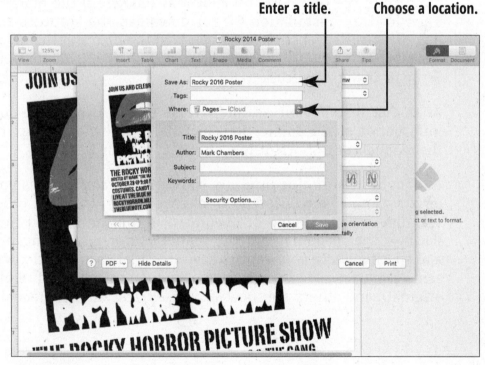

FIGURE 6-3

3. Use the Where pop-up menu to navigate to a folder; then type a filename in the Save As box.

4. Click Save to create your PDF file.

   You can double-click your new PDF file to open it within Preview. Shazam!

Install a USB Scanner

A *scanner* is an external hardware device that you use to import (copy) images to your Mac and "read" text from a page into a Pages or Word file. With a scanner connected to your Mac, you can use the combination of your scanner and printer as a copy machine (with software provided by the manufacturer). If you have a multifunction "all-in-one" printer that scans and faxes as well, you can also perform copy machine and fax machine magic.

Here's just how easy it is to hook up a scanner. As long as your scanner supports OS X El Capitan, plug the USB cable from your scanner into one of the USB ports on your Mac (shown in the margin here). Then load the installation CD (or download the software from the manufacturer's website). After you load the disc and the CD window appears (or the software has been downloaded), double-click the Setup or Install application.

After you install your scanner, refer to the user guide for more information on the applications included by the manufacturer. Often, the manual (or a shortcut to it) is saved to your Desktop.

Although the scanning program you run (and any buttons you press on the scanner) are different for every scanner, the basic process for scanning a paper photo or document is the same: Load the original into the machine, run the manufacturer's scanning program, and specify where you want to save the final scanned file. Note that some scanners act like copy machines (you raise the lid to place the original), and others are sheet-fed (like traditional fax machines).

IN THIS CHAPTER

Explore the Help Window

Search Help

Find Help in the Apple Forums

Share Screens

Search Other Mac Support Resources

Chapter 7

Getting Help

No matter how well written the application or how well designed the operating system, sooner or later, you need support. That goes for everyone from the novice to the experienced Mac owner.

In this short but oh-so-important chapter, I lead you through the various Help resources available on your computer, through Apple, and other suppliers of assistance from sources on the Internet and in your local area.

In this chapter, you find out how to

>> Use the Help resources within El Capitan and Mac applications.

>> Search the El Capitan Help system for specific information.

>> Enable shared screens to allow people to help you by accessing your Mac.

>> Access the Apple online forums and voice support.

>> Get help from third parties.

Explore the Help Window

Your first line of defense for El Capitan is the OS X Mac Help window, as shown in **Figure 7-1**. To display the Help window, go to the Finder menu at the top of your Desktop, click Help, and then choose Mac Help from the drop-down menu. This Help menu is context-sensitive, so it contains menu items that pertain to the application that you're working in.

Toolbar

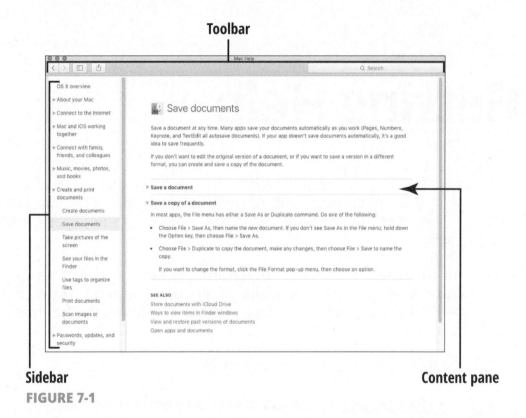

Sidebar

Content pane

FIGURE 7-1

As shown in **Figure 7-1**, the Help window is divided into three sets of controls:

» **Toolbar:** The toolbar includes navigational controls (Back and Forward), a Share button (which allows you to print a topic or send it to someone else via email or social media), the Sidebar button, and the Search Help text box.

» **Sidebar:** Click the Sidebar button on the toolbar to hide or display the sidebar, which offers a selection of the major topics within OS X Help. To show more specific entries under a topic heading, click the triangle next to the heading. To display an entry, just click the entry (much as you click a link in your Safari web browser).

» **Content pane:** This section of the Help window displays the information for the entry you clicked in the sidebar. Again, note that links can appear in the Content pane as well, and you can click one of these links to delve even further into a specific subject.

The Help window might look a daunting at first glance, but when you realize how much information has to be covered to help someone with both a computer and an operating system, you get an idea of why OS X doesn't try to cover everything on one screen. Instead, you get the one tool that does it all: the Search Help box, which I cover in the next section.

Search Help

You have two options when searching for a specific Help topic:

» **From the Finder Help menu:** Wowzers! In El Capitan, you don't even have to open the Help window to search for assistance on a specific topic. Just choose Help from the Finder menu at the top of your Desktop, click the Search field right there on the menu, and type a keyword or two. Topics that El Capitan thinks answer your query start to appear automatically. You don't even need to press Return; just click the topic that sounds the most helpful.

TIP

Although you can ask a full-sentence question, I find that the shorter and more concise your search criteria, the better the relevance of your return.

» **From the Help window:** Click the Search text box on the right side of the Help window toolbar, type one or two words that sum up your question, and press Return. **Figure 7-2** illustrates a typical set of topics concerning USB printers.

Click a topic to read more.　　　　　　　　　　**Type your search term.**

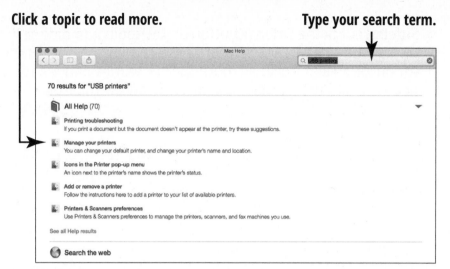

FIGURE 7-2

No matter which method you use, the topics are sorted by approximate relevance first. You can click any topic to display the topic text.

The Help window works much like browsing online: To move back to the previous topic you chose, click the Back button on the Help Center toolbar. (If you're not familiar with the backwards and forwards of web navigation, visit Chapter 14 for all the details.)

Find Help in the Apple Forums

Apple has online product support areas for every hardware and software product it manufactures. Visit www.apple.com, click the Support tab at the top of the web page, and then click the link for your specific Mac model. If you're not sure how to get to www.apple.com, head over to Chapters 13 and 14 to find out how.

The discussion forums hosted by Apple allow Mac owners to provide help and suggestions to help you solve a problem. Apple technicians don't directly answer questions in the forums because technical support isn't free. However, many of the users I've corresponded with over the years seem as knowledgeable as The Paid McCoy!

Click the Support Communities link to display the posting list — the forum shown in **Figure 7-3** covers the Mac Pro computer model — and browse the categories.

Type your search term.

Click to read a discussion.

FIGURE 7-3

To search for specific information in a forum, click the Search or Ask a Question box, type what you're searching for, and then press Return. When you find something of interest, click it to read the question and all the answers. I suggest that you always search before posting a question, because there's usually a good chance that someone else has already posted the same question (and likely received at least one answer).

The forums are message-based, so you may have to read the contents of a complete discussion before you find the solution. Consider it somewhat like panning for gold.

Share Screens

If you've ever leaned on the Mac expert in your family to lead you through the paces of a tricky task — say, adding a second monitor to your system — that's the idea behind the ultimate collaboration tool, *sharing screens.* You can allow someone to remotely control your computer, or you can watch the display on another person's Mac. All it takes is a broadband Internet or local network connection!

The El Capitan screen sharing feature, available from any Finder window, can be turned on for individual users from the Sharing pane in System Preferences. You can allow screen sharing access for all user accounts on your Mac or limit remote access to selected users.

TIP

Sharing a screen with someone you don't absolutely know and trust should set off alarm bells in your cranium. Remember that anyone with shared-screen access can perform most of the same actions that you can, just as though that person were sitting in front of your Mac. Granted, most of the truly devastating things require you to type your admin password, but a malicious individual could still delete files or wreak havoc in any number of ways on your system. Play it smart, and heed this warning: *Be careful with whom you share your screen!*

To set up screen sharing, follow these steps:

1. Click the System Preferences icon on the Dock.

2. Click the Sharing icon to open the Sharing Preferences pane.

3. Select the Screen Sharing check box, as shown in **Figure 7-4**.

   The name is Screen Sharing: On when you have the option selected.

4. To limit remote access for specific user accounts on your Mac, select the Allow Access for Only These Users radio button and then click the Add button (which bears a plus sign) to select a user.

5. Close the System Preferences window to save the change.

Turn on screen sharing.

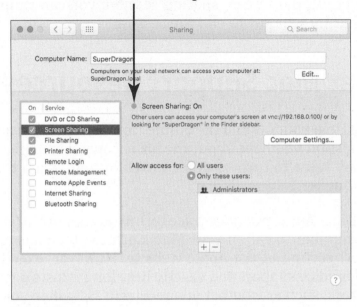

FIGURE 7-4

Now your Mac is ready to share its screen with other Macs. But what if you want to share the screen of another Mac? Naturally, you need to configure that Mac by following the same steps, and it needs to be on your local network.

Once the other Mac is set up for screen sharing, double-click your hard drive icon on your Desktop to open a Finder window; then click the target Mac in the sidebar on the left. (If the Shared section in the sidebar doesn't display the computer's name, hover your pointer over the Shared heading and click Show.)

If both Macs are logged in with the same iCloud account, the sharing session begins immediately. Otherwise, El Capitan requires you to enter a valid user account name and login password for that Mac (just as you specified in Step 4 earlier in this section).

Suddenly, you're seeing the Desktop and applications that the other Mac is running, and you can control the pointer and left- and right-click. *Neat!*

At any time during the screen-sharing session, you can simply close the screen sharing window to end the session.

Search Other Mac Support Resources

Although the Help window and the online forums can take care of just about any question you have about the basic controls and features of OS X, you may want to turn to other forms of help when the going gets a little rougher.

As of this writing, Apple provides voice technical support for OS X. You can find the number to call in your Mac's printed manuals or online in the Support section of the Apple website. However, exactly when you qualify for voice support and exactly how long it lasts depends on different factors, such as whether you received OS X when you bought a new machine or whether you purchased a support plan from Apple.

You can also refer to helpful Mac-savvy publications and resources, both printed and online, for help. My favorites include

> » **Macworld** (www.macworld.com) and **TechRadar** (www.techradar. com), both in oh-so-slick online versions

> » **CNET** (www.cnet.com), an online resource for the latest updates on all sorts of Mac third-party applications

You can also find local resources in any medium-size or large town or city. A shop that's authorized by Apple to sell and repair Mac computers can usually be counted on to answer a quick question over the phone or provide more substantial support for a fee. My local Mac outlet sponsors inexpensive classes for new Mac owners, and if you can reach an Apple Store, the Genius Bar is a useful resource.

You may also be lucky enough to have a local Mac user group that you can join. Its members can be counted on for free answers to your support questions at meetings and demonstrations. To find a group near you, visit the Apple User Groups site at www.apple.com/usergroups, and use the locator.

3
Having Fun and Getting Things Done with Software

Chapter 8

Creating Documents with Pages

Although you're likely familiar with Microsoft Office, you do have another choice when it comes to productivity software on the Mac: Apple's productivity suite can handle similar chores as Word, Excel, and PowerPoint. *Pages,* the page processing program from Apple, handles word processing and desktop publishing, and is available from the App Store free for owners of new Macs.

In this chapter, I show you how to use Pages, including how to

» Create, open, and save Pages documents.

» Use ready-made templates (sample documents) for many different publications.

» Enter and format new text and edit existing text.

» Manipulate text and graphics by using Cut, Copy, and Paste.

» Insert tables, shapes, and photos into your document.

» Spell-check and then print your documents.

Create a New Pages Document

Time to get creative! To start a new Pages document from scratch, follow these steps. And if you want to create your document from a template, I cover that, too. For example, why create a resume or lesson plan from the ground up when a template offers predesigned layout and formatting?

TIP

Pages is free for owners of new Macs. You can download it from the App Store.

1. Click the Launchpad icon on the Dock.

 2. Click the Pages icon.

3. When Pages displays the familiar Open dialog, click the New Document button at the lower-left corner of the dialog. Pages displays the template window you see in **Figure 8-1**.

Select a document type. **Select a template type.**

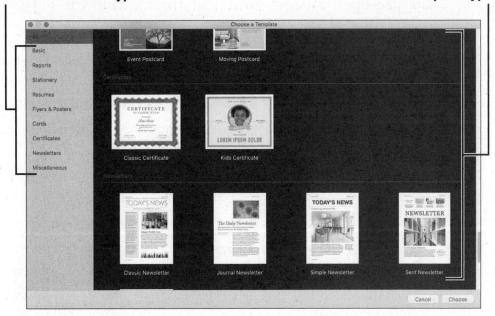

FIGURE 8-1

4. Click to select the type of document you want to create from the list on the left. The document thumbnails on the right are updated with templates that match your choice.

5. Click the template thumbnail that most closely matches your needs.

6. Click Choose to open a new document, using the template you selected.

You can now begin editing, typing new text, and adding graphics (or updating the placeholder graphics in the template), as I illustrate later in the chapter.

Open an Existing Pages Document

Maybe you have a document started, and you want to open it again. You can double-click the document icon in a Finder window. (Chapter 5 explains how to navigate to a file by using the Finder window.) You can also open a Pages document from within the Pages program. Follow these steps:

1. Click the Launchpad icon on the Dock and then click the Pages icon to run the program.

2. Press ⌘+O to display the Open dialog, as shown in **Figure 8-2**.

   The Open dialog operates much like the Finder window; you can even choose the View mode.

Select a drive.   **Double-click the filename.**

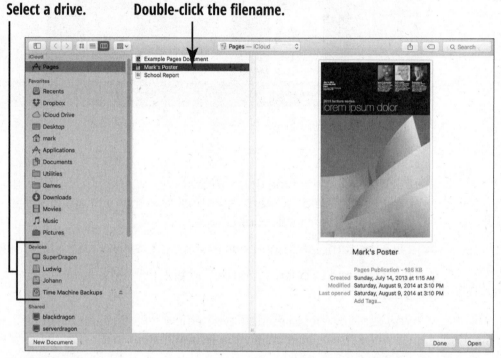

FIGURE 8-2

3. Click to select a hard drive on the Devices list on the left side of the dialog; then click (or double-click, depending on the View mode) folders and subfolders until you locate the Pages document.

TIP

By default, Pages saves its document files in your iCloud Drive, allowing you to open a Pages document using iOS devices (like your iPad) or other Macs. You can always easily reach the contents of your iCloud Drive from any Finder window; just click the iCloud Drive entry in the Favorites section on the left side of the window.

4. Double-click the filename to open it.

Type and Edit Text within Pages

Typing in a word processor is similar to typing on a typewriter, but you need to know a few ways in which word processors are unique. If you're a newcomer to the world of word processing, you find the basics in this section. Here's what you need to know to get started:

» The bar-shaped text cursor, which looks like a capital letter *I*, indicates where the text you enter will appear within a Pages document. You control the placement of the cursor by using the arrow keys on your keyboard. Or just click with the mouse where you want to place the cursor.

» Then, to enter text, simply begin typing where the cursor is.

TIP

Unlike with a typewriter, you don't need to press Return at the edge of the page. The software wraps the text to a new line for you. The only time to press Return is when you want to start a new paragraph.

» To edit text in your Pages document, click the insertion cursor at any point in the text and drag the insertion cursor across the characters to highlight them. Then type the replacement text. Pages automatically replaces the existing characters with the ones you type. You can see selected text (*Project Proposal*) in **Figure 8-3**.

» To delete text, highlight the characters and then press Delete.

TIP

Simple character–by–character editing works well with smaller blocks of text. If you have a bigger editing job, you can certainly move a larger block of text from one part of your Pages document to another. Or perhaps you want to copy a block to a second location. That's when you can call on the power of the Cut, Copy, and Paste features within Pages. The next few sections explain how to perform these actions.

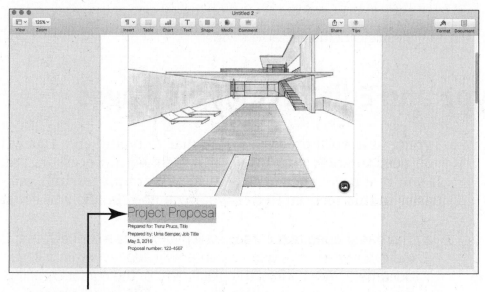

This text is selected.

FIGURE 8-3

Cut Text

You can easily cut selected text or graphics to remove them from your document. If you simply want to remove the selected material from your Pages document (and you don't plan to paste it somewhere else), just select the text and press the Delete key.

Or, if you want, you can save what you cut and place it on your Clipboard so that you can use that text or graphics in something else. Think of the Clipboard as a temporary holding area.

To cut text or graphics and place that material on the Clipboard, first make your selection. Then do one of the following:

» Choose Edit ➪ Cut.

» Press ⌘+X.

Don't forget: Your Clipboard can hold only one cut's worth of data at a time, so if you cut another selection of text or another graphic, you'll lose what you originally had on the Clipboard.

Copy Text

When you copy text or graphics, the original selection remains untouched, but a copy of the selection is automatically placed on the Clipboard. Select some text or graphics and do one of the following:

» Choose Edit ➪ Copy.

» Press ⌘+C.

Cutting or copying a new selection to the Clipboard erases what was there. In other words, the Clipboard holds only the latest material you cut or copied.

Paste from the Clipboard

After you have something copied to your Clipboard — no matter whether you made a Cut or a Copy — you can paste it wherever you want. You can repeat a paste operation as often as you like because the contents of the Clipboard aren't cleared as soon as you paste something. Having said that, though, remember that because the Clipboard holds the contents of only your *last* Copy or Cut operation, you must paste that content before you cut or copy again; otherwise, you'll lose that content from the Clipboard.

To paste the Clipboard contents, click the insertion cursor at the location you want and then do one of the following:

» Choose Edit ➪ Paste.

» Press ⌘+V.

Format Text with Panache

If you feel that some (or all) of the text in your Pages document needs a facelift, you can format that text any way you like. Formatting lets you change the color, font family, character size, and attributes as necessary. And unlike using a typewriter, where you have to decide ahead of time what you want to boldface or italicize, you can format your text after you write it.

TIP

First, of course, you must select some text. Just click and drag the cursor over the text you want to select, and release the mouse (or trackpad) when you're done. To select all text in a document — say, you want to change the font from something boring to something jazzy for an invitation — press ⌘+A.

You can apply basic formatting in two ways:

» **Use the Format drawer.** The Format drawer appears on the right side of the Pages window, as shown in **Figure 8-4**. (If you don't see the Format drawer, click the Format button on the Pages toolbar, which carries a paintbrush icon.) Click one of the rectangular tabs at the top of the Format drawer to display the settings for that category. If you click the Text tab and then click the Font drop-down menu button, for example, you can change the font family from Arial to a more daring font. You can also select characteristics such as the font's color (perfect for highlighting items) or choose italic or boldface. The Format drawer also provides buttons for font alignment (Align Left, Center, Align Right, and Justify).

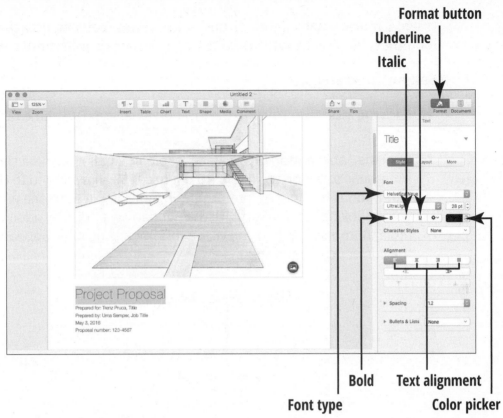

Format button

Underline

Italic

Bold

Text alignment

Font type

Color picker

FIGURE 8-4

» **Use the Format menu.** Most controls in the Format drawer are also available on the Format menu. Click Format and hover your cursor over the Font menu item, and you can apply boldface, italic, and underline to the selected text. You can also make the text bigger (great for headlines) or smaller (for a caption). To change the alignment from the Format menu, click Format and hover the mouse cursor over the Text menu item.

Insert Tables

In the world of word processing, a *table* is a grid that holds text or graphics for easy comparison — for example, comparing the features and prices of similar products in a brochure or creating a simple travel itinerary with dates, times, and events. You can create a spiffy-looking table layout within Pages with a few simple mouse clicks.

Follow these steps:

1. Click the insertion cursor at the location where you want the table to appear.

2. Click the Table button on the Pages toolbar. Pages displays a simple thumbnail selection tool (visible in **Figure 8-5**), allowing you to click a thumbnail to choose a preformatted table. If you don't see what you're looking for, you can click the right arrow to display additional table thumbnails. When you click a thumbnail, the table appears at the current cursor location.

Click to create a table.

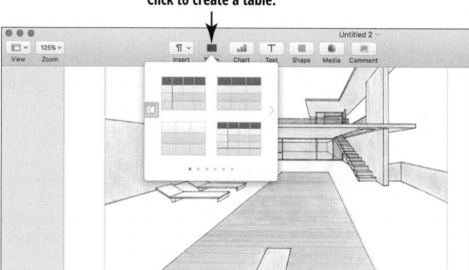

FIGURE 8-5

3. Click within a cell in the table, and enter its text. The table cell automatically resizes and wraps the text you enter to fit.

You can paste material from the Clipboard into a table. See "Paste from the Clipboard" earlier in this chapter for details on pasting.

TIP

4. To change the borders of a cell, click the cell to select it, click the Cell tab in the Format drawer, and then click one of the Border buttons to change the border.

Select multiple cells in a table by holding down Shift while you click.

5. To add a background color (or even fill cells with an image for a background), click the Cell tab in the Format drawer, and choose a type of background from the Fill section.

6. To return to editing text, simply click within the document anywhere outside the table.

Add Photos

When you want to add a picture to your document, you can add it in either of two ways: as a *floating* object (which you place in a particular spot from which it doesn't move, even if you make changes to the text) or as an *inline* object (which flows with the surrounding text as you make layout changes).

» **Add a floating object.** Drag an image file from a Finder window and place it at the spot you want within your document. Alternatively, you can click the Media button on the toolbar and then choose Photos, which takes you to the *Media Browser,* which displays images from Photos, as well as other locations on your Mac. Navigate to where the file is saved, and drag the image thumbnail to the spot you want to place the image in the document. **Figure 8-6** illustrates the Media Browser in action.

You can send a floating object (such as a shape or an image) to the *background,* where text doesn't wrap around it. To bring back a background object as a regular floating object, click the object to select it and choose Arrange ➪ Bring to Front. (I tell you more about background objects later in this chapter.)

FIGURE 8-6

» **Add an inline object.** Hold down the Command (⌘) key while you drag an image file from a Finder window and place the image where you want within your document. You can also click the Media button and choose Photos to display the Media Browser. Navigate to the location where the file is saved, hold down the ⌘ key, and drag the image thumbnail to the spot where you want to place it in the document.

To move an image, click it to select it and then drag it to the new location within your document.

Resize an Image

Okay, you've added an image to your Pages document, but it's way too small or too big. This problem is easily fixed, though, because you can resize the image at any time. To resize an image object, follow these steps:

1. Click the image to select it.

2. Drag one of the selection handles (the tiny white squares) that appear along the border of the image. There are two kinds of these handles. The *side-selection* handles drag only that edge of the frame, and the *corner-selection* handles resize both adjoining edges of the selection frame. **Figure 8-7** shows an image that I'm resizing in a document.

Side selection handles

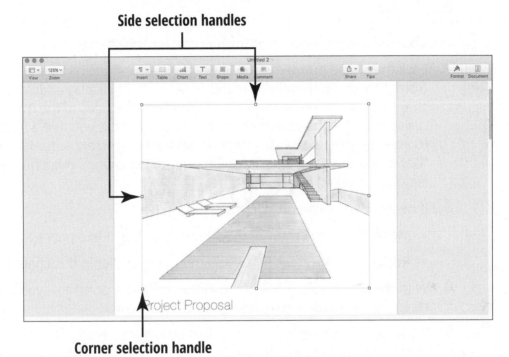

Corner selection handle

FIGURE 8-7

 TIP Hold down the Shift key while you drag, and Pages preserves the aspect ratio of the image so that the vertical and horizontal proportions remain fixed. (Otherwise, your image might look stretched or distorted.)

 TIP You can also flip images. With the image still selected, click Arrange on the Pages menu bar to flip the image horizontally or vertically.

Add a Shape to the Document Background

Need to add a shape as a visual border to your newsletter page or perhaps as a background for a customer's quote in your brochure? To add a shape (such as a rectangle or circle) to your document, follow these steps:

1. Click the insertion cursor in the location for the shape.

2. Click the Shape button on the Pages toolbar, and click on a shape from the pop-up thumbnail menu to select it. To display additional shapes, click the left and right arrow icons at the sides of the thumbnail menu. The shape appears in your document. If you add a shape to an area with text (or drag it into a text area), the text automatically "flows" around the shape. (More about how to change this in just a sentence or two.)

3. If needed, you can resize or move the shape:

   - **Move:** Click the center of the shape, and drag it to a new spot.

   - **Resize:** See the steps in "Resize an Image" earlier in this chapter.

4. With the shape selected — the handles appear around it — you can click in the Format drawer and choose the fill color.

5. When your shape is in place, add text atop it (rather than allow the text to flow around it) by selecting the shape, choosing Arrange ⇨ Send to Back, and then typing the text.

Check Your Spelling

Pages can check spelling while you type (the default setting) or check it after you complete your document. If you find automatic spell checking distracting, you should definitely pick the latter method.

To check spelling as you type, follow these steps:

1. Click Edit on the Pages menu bar, and hover your cursor over the Spelling and Grammar menu item.

2. Click Check Spelling While Typing. If a possible misspelling is found, Pages underlines the word with a red dashed line.

3. You can right-click a possibly misspelled word to choose a possible correct spelling from the list, or you can ignore the word if it's spelled correctly.

TIP

To turn off automatic spell checking, click the Check Spelling While Typing menu item again to disable it. The check mark next to the menu item disappears.

To check spelling manually, follow these steps:

1. Click within the document to place the text insertion cursor where the spell check should begin.

2. Click Edit, hover your cursor over the Spelling and Grammar menu item, and choose Check Document Now.

3. Right-click any possible misspellings and choose the correct spelling, or choose Ignore Spelling if the word is spelled correctly.

Find and Replace Text

If you're working with an existing document, why scan several pages looking for a specific word or phrase when you can use the Find command? Pages can locate a word or phrase and show you every occurrence within your document.

To find (and optionally replace) a target word or phrase, follow these steps:

1. Click Edit on the Pages menu bar, hover your cursor over the Find menu item, and click Find.

2. When the Find dialog appears, type the word or phrase you want to locate in the Find text box. If any matches are found, they are highlighted in your Pages document; the number of matches is displayed in the Find & Replace dialog box.

TIP

Pages will search for an exact match, so type only the exact word or phrase you want.

3. To replace a word or phrase throughout the document, click the Action drop-down menu at the left of the Find Text box and choose Find & Replace from the menu. Now you can enter both the original text (in the Find text box) and the replacement text (in the Replace text box). You can choose to replace all occurrences, or use the Forward and Back arrows to move between occurrences and replace them individually.

Print Documents

Ready to start the presses? You can print your Pages document on real paper, of course, but don't forget that you can save a tree by creating an electronic PDF-format document rather than a printout.

TIP

A *PDF* file is sort of an electronic printout. I show you how to create a PDF in Chapter 6. PDF documents can be easily displayed within El Capitan, or you can use the free Acrobat Reader from Adobe (`http://get.adobe.com/reader`) to view your work.

To print your Pages document on old-fashioned paper, follow these steps:

1. Within Pages, click File and choose Print. Pages displays the Print sheet you see in **Figure 8-8**.

2. Click in the Copies field, and enter the number of copies you need.

3. Select the pages to print.

   - *To print the entire document,* select All.

   - *To print a range of selected pages,* select the From radio button and then enter the starting and ending pages.

4. Click the Print button to send the document to your default printer.

Change the number of copies you want to print and the page range.

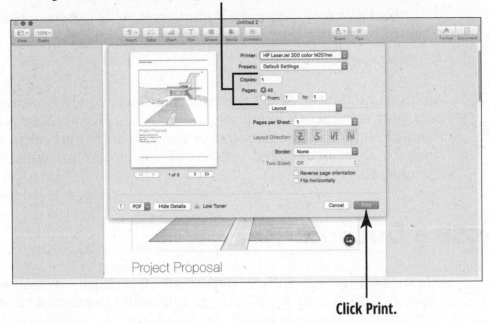

Click Print.

FIGURE 8-8

Save Your Work

To save a Pages document after you finish it (or to take a break while designing), follow these steps within Pages:

1. If you're saving a document that hasn't yet been saved, press ⌘+S or choose File ⇨ Save. The Save sheet you see in **Figure 8-9** appears.

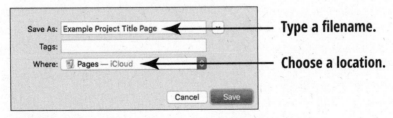

Type a filename.

Choose a location.

FIGURE 8-9

2. Type a filename for your new document.

3. Choose a location to save the document. By default, Pages saves your document to the Pages folder in your iCloud Drive.

4. Click Save.

TIP

After you fill out the Save sheet and click Save, your Mac remembers your document's filename and location. If you make additional changes to a document after you save it, simply press ⌘+S again to save an updated version of the document with your changes. You're done!

Close a Document

When you're done with a document, you have several ways to close that document (and then open another document or quit the application). Simply do one of the following:

» Choose File ➪ Close. Pages stays running, and the Pages menu bar is still visible.

» Press ⌘+W, which is the same as the Close menu command.

» Click the red Close button on the Pages toolbar. Again, Pages stays running, so you can open another document.

» Choose File ➪ Quit. Pages closes the current document and quits.

» Press ⌘+Q, which is the same as the Quit menu command.

Chapter 9
Working with Numbers

Oh, heavens, it's a spreadsheet! That immediately means that it's complex, right? Actually, Numbers is the easiest spreadsheet program I've ever used for such tasks as arranging numbers, forecasting important numeric trends, and taking care of a household budget. And unlike the Microsoft Office spreadsheet application (Excel) — which many folks find just too doggone powerful and confusing — Numbers is specifically designed with the home Mac owner in mind.

In this chapter, I provide the explanations and procedures you need to begin using Numbers. You see how to

» Create, open, and save new Numbers spreadsheets.

» Enter and edit data in a cell.

» Format cells.

» Add and remove rows and columns.

» Create simple calculations.

» Insert charts into your document.

Understand Spreadsheets

A *spreadsheet* simply organizes and calculates numbers by using a grid system of rows and columns. The intersection of each row and column is a *cell*, and cells can hold either text or numeric values (along with calculations that are usually linked to the contents of other, surrounding cells).

Spreadsheets are wonderful tools for making decisions and comparisons because they let you "plug in" different numbers — such as interest rates or your monthly insurance premium — and instantly see the results. Some of my favorite spreadsheets that I use regularly include

» Car and mortgage loan comparisons

» A college planner

» My household budget (not that we pay any attention to it, but it makes me feel better)

TIP Numbers is available free from the Apple App Store for owners of new Macs.

Create a New Spreadsheet

To create a new spreadsheet within Numbers, follow these steps:

1. Click the Launchpad icon on the Dock.

2. Click the Numbers icon.

3. In the Open dialog, click the New Document button. Numbers displays the template dialog you see in **Figure 9-1**.

Select a document type.   Select a template.

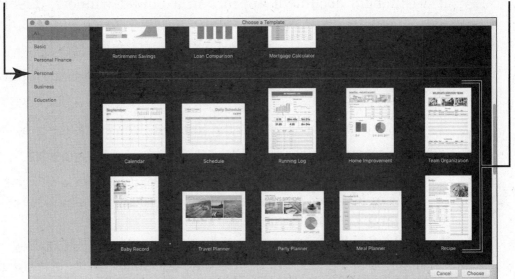

FIGURE 9-1

4. Click the type of document you want to create from the list on the left. The document thumbnails on the right are updated with templates that match your choice.

I was pleasantly surprised when I ran Numbers the first time: A glance at the supplied templates proves that Apple has targeted the home Mac owner. After making a few modifications, you can easily use the Budget, Personal Budget, and Mortgage Calculator templates to create your own spreadsheets, for example.

5. Click the template that most closely matches your needs. (You can also choose the Blank thumbnail to start a Numbers spreadsheet from scratch.)

6. Click the Choose button to open a new document, using the template you selected.

Open an Existing Spreadsheet

If a Numbers document appears in a Finder window, double-click the document icon; Numbers automatically loads and displays the spreadsheet.

To open a Numbers document from within the program, follow these steps:

1. From within Launchpad, click the Numbers icon to run the program.

2. Press ⌘+O to display the Open dialog, as shown in **Figure 9-2**.

You can toggle View mode in the Open dialog, just like in a Finder window. (Chapter 3 discusses each of the Finder View modes.) In **Figure 9-2**, I'm using Icon view mode.

3. Click to select a drive from the Devices list on the left side of the dialog, and then click (or double-click, depending on the View mode you're using) folders and subfolders until you locate the desired Numbers document.

4. Double-click the spreadsheet to load it.

To open a spreadsheet you've been working on the past few days, choose File⇨Open Recent to display Numbers documents that you worked on recently.

Find the folder where your spreadsheet is stored.

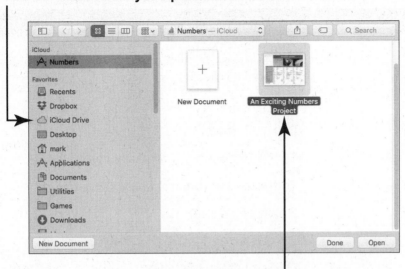

Double-click the file you want to open.

FIGURE 9-2

TIP

You can also select other locations from the list on the left side of the Open dialog. Click iCloud Drive to view all the documents you've saved within iCloud online, for example, or click the Documents icon in the list to jump directly to your Documents folder.

Navigate and Select Cells in a Spreadsheet

Before you can enter data into a cell, you need to know how to reach the cell where you want to enter the data. You can use the scroll bars to move around in your spreadsheet, but when you enter data into cells, moving your fingers from the keyboard is a hassle. For this reason, Numbers has several movement shortcut keys that you can use to navigate. I list those keys in Table 9-1. After you commit these keys to memory, your productivity shoots straight to the top.

TABLE 9-1 **Movement Shortcut Keys in Numbers**

Key or Key Combination	Where the Cursor Moves
Left arrow (←)	One cell to the left
Right arrow (→)	One cell to the right
Up arrow (↑)	One cell up
Down arrow (↓)	One cell down
Option+Fn+←	To the beginning of the active worksheet
Option+Fn+→	To the end of the active worksheet
Page Down	Down one screen
Page Up	Up one screen
Return	One cell down (also works within a selection)
Tab	One cell to the right (also works within a selection)
Shift+Enter	One cell up (also works within a selection)
Shift+Tab	One cell to the left (also works within a selection)

You can use your mouse or trackpad to select cells in a spreadsheet:

» To select a *single* cell, click it.

» To select a *range* of multiple adjacent cells, click a cell at any corner of the range you want and then drag the cursor in the direction you want (see **Figure 9-3**).

» To select nonadjacent cells, hold down the Command (⌘) key while you click each cell.

» To select a *column* of cells, click the alphabetic heading button at the top of the column.

» To select a *row* of cells, click the numeric heading button at the far-left end of the row.

A	B	C	D	E	F
		Table 1			
	Monday	Tuesday	Wednesday	Thursday	Friday
Group A	$2251.00	$1786.24	$7339.00	$5468.71	$1212.30
Group B	$5458.25	$8852.00	$55.00	$77.00	$4777.00
Group C	$3125.00	$855.00	$7999.34	$4418.00	$882.00

A selected range of cells

FIGURE 9-3

Enter and Edit Data in a Spreadsheet

After you navigate to the cell in which you want data to be, you're ready to enter it. The following steps walk you through the key tasks:

1. Click the cell or press the spacebar. A cursor appears, indicating that the cell is ready to hold any data you type.

2. Type your data. Spreadsheets can use both numbers and text within a cell; either type of information is considered to be data in the spreadsheet world. You can see data being entered in **Figure 9-4**.

Don't forget that you can copy data from another document (using ⌘+C) and paste that data into the cell (using ⌘+V).

TIP

Group C	$3125.00
Group D	3837.00

FIGURE 9-4

3. To correct or edit data, click within the cell that contains the data to select it and then click the cell again to display the insertion cursor. Drag the insertion cursor across the characters to highlight them and then type the replacement data.

TIP

Numbers automatically replaces the existing characters with those you type.

4. To delete text, highlight the characters and then press Delete.

5. When you're ready to move on, press Return (to save the data and move one cell down) or press Tab (to save the data and move one cell to the right).

Choose a Number Format

After your data has been entered into a cell, row, or column, you may need to format it. *Number formatting* determines how a cell displays a number, such as a dollar amount, a percentage, or a date. Characters and formatting rules, such as decimal places, commas, and dollar and percentage notation, are included in number formatting. So if your spreadsheet contains units of currency, such as dollars, format it that way. Then all you need to do is type the numbers; the currency formatting is applied automatically.

Numbers gives you a healthy selection of formatting possibilities. To specify a number format, follow these steps:

1. Select the cells, rows, or columns you want to format. (See "Navigate and Select Cells in a Spreadsheet," earlier in this chapter, for tips.)

2. Click the Format toolbar button at the right end of the Numbers toolbar to display the Format drawer.

3. Click the Cell tab in the Format drawer to display the settings you see in **Figure 9-5**.

4. Click the Data Format pop-up menu, and choose the type of formatting you want to apply.

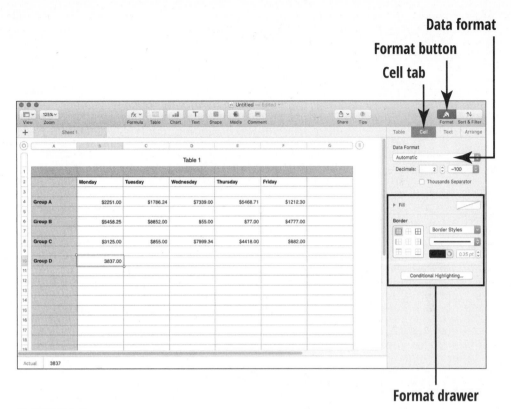

FIGURE 9-5

Change the Cell Text Alignment

You can change the alignment of text in selected cells. (The default alignment for text is flush left.) Follow these steps:

1. Select the cells, rows, or columns you want to format. (See the task "Navigate and Select Cells in a Spreadsheet," earlier in this chapter, for tips.)

2. Click the Format toolbar button.

3. Click the Text tab to display the settings you see in **Figure 9-6**.

4. Click the corresponding alignment button to choose the type of formatting you want to apply. (You can choose left, right, center, justified, or text left and numbers right.) Text can also be aligned at the top, center, or bottom of a cell.

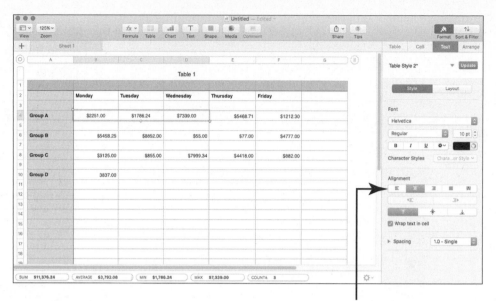

Alignment buttons

FIGURE 9-6

Change Character Formatting

You may need to set apart the contents of some cells, perhaps to create text headings for some columns and rows or to highlight the totals in a spreadsheet. Follow these steps to change the formatting of the data displayed within selected cells:

1. Select the cells, rows, or columns you want to format. (See "Navigate and Select Cells in a Spreadsheet," earlier in this chapter, for tips.)

2. Click the Format button.

3. Click the Text tab to display the settings shown in **Figure 9-7**.

4. Click the Font pop-up menu, the up and down arrows next to the Font Size box, or Font Color button in the Format drawer to format the text.

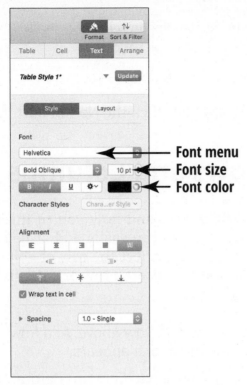

Font menu

Font size

Font color

FIGURE 9-7

Format with Shading

Shading the contents of a cell, row, or column is helpful when your spreadsheet contains subtotals or logical divisions. Follow these steps to shade cells, rows, or columns by using the Fill feature:

1. Select the cells, rows, or columns you want to format. (See the task "Navigate and Select Cells in a Spreadsheet," earlier in this chapter, for tips.)

2. Click the Format toolbar button.

3. Click the Cell tab button within the Format drawer.

4. Click the color box next to the Fill heading to select the shading and color option. Numbers displays a color picker dialog.

5. Click to select a color, gradient, or image fill.

TIP

To remove any fill previously applied, click the No Fill button.

Insert and Delete Rows and Columns

What's that? You forgot to add a row, and now you're three pages into your data entry? No problem. You can easily add or delete rows and columns. Really — you can! First, select the row or column that you want to delete or that you want to insert a row or column next to. Then do one of the following:

» **For a row:** Right-click and choose Add Row Above, Add Row Below, or Delete Row from the menu that appears.

» **For a column:** Right-click and choose Add Columns Before, Add Columns After, or Delete Column from the menu that appears.

TIP

You can also take care of this business from the Table menu. After you select the row or column, click Table and then choose any of the menu items: Add Rows, Add Columns, Delete Rows, or Delete Columns. (Personally, I like to right–click.)

Add Simple Calculations

It's time to talk about *formulas.* These equations calculate values based on the contents of cells you specify in your spreadsheet. If you designate cell A1 (the cell in column A at row 1) to hold your yearly salary and cell B1 to hold the number 12, you can divide the contents of cell A1 by cell B1 (to calculate your monthly salary) by typing this formula in any other cell:

```
=A1/B1
```

TIP

By the way, formulas in Numbers always start with an equal sign (=).

So why not just use a calculator? Maybe you want to calculate your weekly salary. Rather than grab a pencil and paper, you can simply change the contents of cell B1 to 52, and — boom! — the spreadsheet is updated to display your weekly salary.

That's a simple example, of course, but it demonstrates the basis of using formulas (and the reason why spreadsheets are often used to predict trends and forecast budgets).

To add a simple formula within your spreadsheet, follow these steps:

1. Click inside the cell that will hold the result of your calculation and type = (an equal sign). The Formula bar appears along either side of the cell.

2. Click the Format button on the toolbar. The Functions display appears at the right side of the window, as shown in **Figure 9-8.**

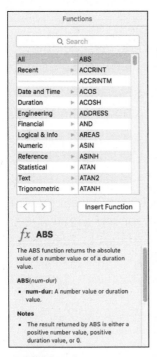

FIGURE 9-8

3. Click a function to display additional information about the function. This list makes it easier to choose among the wide range of functions available within Numbers.

4. When you've selected the desired function, click the Insert Function button to add the function to the Formula bar.

5. After you finish inserting functions, click the Accept button on the Formula bar (which bears a green check mark) to add the formula to the cell. Now Excel is ready to work behind the scenes, doing math for you so that the correct numbers appear in the cell.

Insert Charts

Sometimes, you just have to see something to believe it — hence, the ability to use the data you add to a spreadsheet to generate a professional–looking chart! Follow these steps to create a chart:

1. Select the adjacent cells you want to chart by clicking and dragging the mouse or trackpad.

   To choose individual cells that aren't adjacent, you can hold down the ⌘ key as you click.

TIP

2. Click the Chart button on the Numbers toolbar, which looks like a bar graph. Numbers displays the thumbnail menu you see in **Figure 9-9**.

3. Click the thumbnail for the chart type you want. Numbers inserts the chart as an object within your spreadsheet so that you can move the chart or resize it just like an object in Pages.

   Numbers also displays the Chart settings in the Format drawer, where you can change the colors and add (or remove) the chart title and legend. **Figure 9-10** illustrates a simple chart I added to a spreadsheet, complete with the Chart settings in the Format drawer. The chart appears in the bottom-left corner of the figure (surrounded by resizing handles).

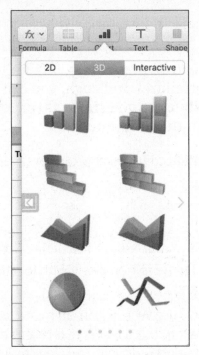

FIGURE 9-9

Selected cells

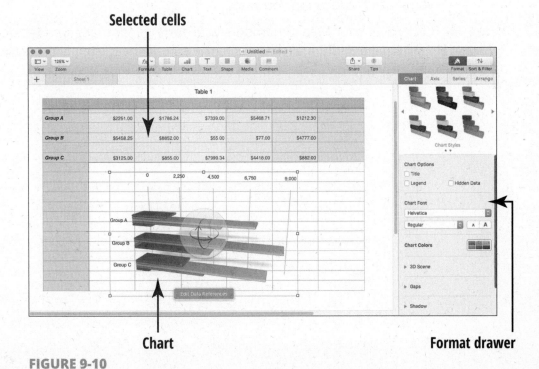

Chart

Format drawer

FIGURE 9-10

Save Your Work

Although El Capitan's Auto Save feature prevents you from losing a significant chunk of work to power failures and such, you can always save a Numbers document manually after you finish it (or to save it for later). Follow these steps within the program:

1. Press ⌘+S. If you're saving a document that hasn't yet been saved, the Save As sheet appears.

2. Type a filename for the new document.

3. From the Where pop-up menu, choose a location to save the document. (This step lets you select common locations, like your Desktop, iCloud Drive, Documents folder or Home folder, along with locations you saved other documents to recently.)

TIP

If the location you want isn't listed on the Where pop-up menu, you can click the down-arrow button next to the Save As text box to display the full Save As dialog. Click to select a drive in the Devices list on the left side of the dialog; then click folders and subfolders until you reach the location you want.

4. Click Save. Your Mac remembers your settings for that spreadsheet. If you make additional changes to the spreadsheet, simply press ⌘+S and your changes are saved as a new version of the document.

Chapter 10

Getting the Most from Photos

I t's no accident that Macs are the "tool of choice" for photographers around the world!

By designing hardware and software crafted to work smoothly together — along with the intuitive look and feel of OS X — Apple lets you easily organize and produce your own multimedia with digital tools like Photos.

You can use Apple's Photos application to

» Transfer photos from your digital camera to your Mac.

» Send photos to others by email.

» Tag your photos with keywords to help keep your collection organized.

» Edit photos to improve their appearance.

Upload Pictures from Your Digital Camera

Photos makes it easy to download images directly from your digital camera — as long as your specific camera model is supported in Photos, that is. Most cameras are supported, though, and more are added to the supported crowd during every update. You can also connect your iPhone to your Mac using the cable supplied by Apple, and the import procedure is the same.

Follow these steps to import images:

1. Connect your digital camera to your Mac and then turn on the camera.

Plug one end of a USB cable into your camera and the other end into your Mac's USB port, and prepare your camera to download images.

2. Launch Photos.

Your Mac will probably launch Photos automatically when your camera is connected, but you can always launch Photos manually by clicking its icon on the Dock (or by clicking the Photos icon in Launchpad). Depending on your camera model, Photos may automatically display the Import pane, but if you don't see the title Import at the top of the Photos window, click the Import button on the toolbar.

3. Specify whether the images you're importing should be deleted from the camera afterward.

If you don't expect to download these images again to another computer or another device, you can choose to delete the photos from your camera automatically by clicking the Delete Items After Import check box to enable it. (This way, you save a step and help eliminate the guilt that can crop up when you nix your pix. Sorry, I couldn't resist.) If you'd rather be absolutely certain that everything has been imported safely, leave the check box disabled, allowing you to delete the images from your camera manually.

4. Click the Import All New Photos button to import your photographs from the camera.

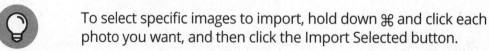

To select specific images to import, hold down ⌘ and click each photo you want, and then click the Import Selected button.

TIP

The images are added to your Photo Library, where you can organize them into individual albums. (More on albums later.) Depending on the camera, Photos may also import video clips.

You're probably familiar with albums, which you may recognize from older versions of Photos. An *album* is simply a container you create in Photos that contains specific photos; it's straightforward. Typical albums might include family pets or photos of your hometown.

Photos also offers three viewing modes — called *Moments*, *Collections*, and *Years* — that help you view photos by date. When you display your library in Moments view, Photos displays sets of images taken at about the same time, in the same location. In Collections view, photos are grouped by locations and dates that are relatively close together. Finally, in Year view, photos are grouped by the year they were taken. Think about that: Arranging old-fashioned film prints by the moments and events they document is tough, but Photos makes it easy!

To view photos by Moments, Collections, or Years, click the Photos button on the toolbar. You can switch among Years, Collections, and Moments views by clicking the Forward and Back arrows in the upper-left corner of the Photos window.

IMPORTING IMAGES FROM YOUR HARD DRIVE

If you have a folder of images that you've already collected on your Mac's hard drive, a CD or DVD, an external drive, or a USB flash drive, adding them to your library is easy. Just drag the folder from a Finder window and drop it into the list in the Photos window sidebar. You can sit back while the images are imported into your library. Photos recognizes images in several formats: GIF, JPEG, PSD, PICT, PNG, RAW, and TIFF.

If you have individual images, you can drag them as well. Select the images in a Finder window and drag them into an album in the sidebar (or drop them directly in the Viewer).

If you'd rather import images by using a standard OS X Open dialog, choose File ➪ Import to Library. Simplicity strikes again!

Display a Digital Image in Photos

Say goodbye to the old shoebox full of slides and prints! Browsing your Photos library is as simple as clicking these items:

» A specific album in the sidebar, as shown in **Figure 10-1**

» The Photos item in the sidebar (or the Photos button on the toolbar), which displays your photos in Moments or Years view

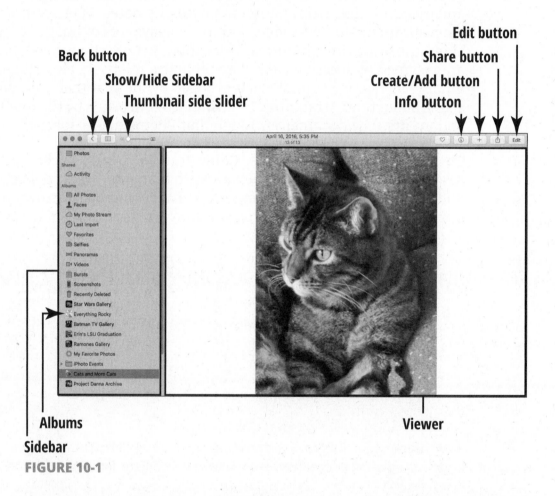

FIGURE 10-1

Drag the scroll button on the scroll bar to move up or down, or click a specific photo and use the arrow keys to navigate your collection.

After you locate the image you want to see, you can double-click it to display the photo within the Photos window.

To view the photo full-screen, click it to select it and press ⌘+Control+F. You can leave Full Screen mode at any time by pressing Esc.

TIP

While in Full Screen mode, move your cursor to the top edge of the screen to display the Photos menu bar (see **Figure 10-2**), which allows you to choose menu commands without exiting.

Photos menu bar

FIGURE 10-2

Tag Your Photos with Keywords

"Okay, Mark, albums are great, but do you really expect me to look through 20 albums just to locate pictures with specific people or places?" Never fear, good Mac owner. You can also assign descriptive *keywords* to images to help you organize your collection and locate certain pictures fast. Photos comes with several standard keywords, and you can create your own as well.

Suppose that you want to identify your images according to special events in your family. Birthday photos should have their own keywords, and anniversaries deserve another. By assigning keywords, you can search for Elsie's sixth birthday or your silver wedding anniversary (no matter which album they're in), and all related photos with those keywords appear like magic! (Well, *almost* like magic. You need to choose View➪Metadata➪Keywords, which toggles the Keyword display on and off in the Viewer.)

Photos includes these keywords, which are already available:

» Birthday

» Checkmark

» Family

» Favorite

» Flagged

» Movie

» Kids

» Photo Booth

» Photo Stream

» Vacation

» RAW

TIP

The Checkmark keyword comes in handy for temporarily identifying specific images because you can search for just the checkmarked photos. Say that you're searching for 12 great shots for a custom calendar. You can Checkmark those shots temporarily to mark them, and you can remove the check mark when the calendar is finished.

To assign keywords to images (or remove keywords that have already been assigned), select one or more photos in the Viewer. Choose Window➪Keyword Manager or press ⌘+K to display the Keywords window, as shown in **Figure 10-3**. Adding any keyword displays a tiny tag icon in the lower-left corner of the image.

Click a button to assign a keyword.

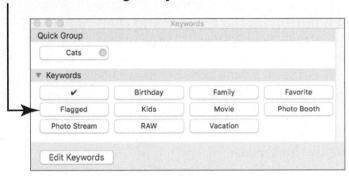

FIGURE 10-3

Click the keyword buttons that you want to attach to the selected images to mark them. Or click the highlighted keyword buttons that you want to remove from the selected images to disable them. You can assign as many keywords to a photo as you like.

YOU'RE GONNA NEED YOUR OWN KEYWORDS

I would bet that you take photos of subjects other than just kids and vacations, and that's why Photos lets you create your own keywords. Display the Photos Keywords window by pressing ⌘+K, click the Edit Keywords button, and then click Add (the button with the plus sign). Photos adds a new, unnamed keyword to the list as an edit box, ready for you to type its name.

You can rename an existing keyword from the same window. Click a keyword to select it and then click Rename. Remember, however, that renaming a keyword affects *all images tagged with that keyword*, even if the new keyword no longer applies to the photos. That might be confusing when, for example, photos originally tagged as Family suddenly appear with the keyword Foodstuffs because you renamed the keyword. (I recommend applying a new keyword and deleting the old one if this problem crops up.)

To change the keyboard shortcut assigned to a keyword, click the Shortcut button. To remove an existing keyword from the list, click the keyword to select it and then click the Delete button, which bears a minus sign.

To sift through your entire collection of images by using keywords, click the Search button on the toolbar and then type the desired keyword. (You can search for multiple keywords by separating them with spaces.)

TIP

The images that remain in the Viewer after a search must have *all* the keywords you specified. If an image is identified by only three of four keywords you chose, for example, it isn't a match, and it doesn't appear in the Viewer.

Organize Photos in Albums

The basic organizational tool in Photos is the *album.* Each album can represent any division you like, whether it's a year, a vacation, your daughter, or your daughter's ex-boyfriends. Follow these steps:

1. Create a new album by choosing File ➪ New Album or pressing ⌘+N.

The New Album sheet appears (as shown in **Figure 10-4**).

FIGURE 10-4

2. Click in the Album Name box and type the name for your new photo album.

3. Press Return. The new album appears under the Albums heading in the sidebar. You can drag images from the Viewer into any album you choose. You can copy an image to another album by dragging it from the Viewer to an album in the sidebar, for example.

To remove a photo that has fallen out of favor, follow these steps:

1. In the sidebar, select an album.

2. In the Viewer, click to select the photo you want to remove.

3. Press Delete.

When you remove a photo from an album, you *don't* remove the photo from your collection (represented by the Photos entry in the sidebar or the Photos button on the toolbar). That's because an album is just a group of links to the images in your collection. To remove the offending photo, click the Photos entry in the sidebar to display your entire collection of images, and delete the picture there. (Naturally, this also removes the photo from any albums that may have contained it as well.)

To remove an entire album from the sidebar, just click to select it in the sidebar — in the Viewer, you can see the images it contains — and then press Delete.

To rename an album, click to select the entry under the Albums heading in the sidebar and then click again to display a text box. Type the new album name and then press Return.

Create a Slide Show

You can use Photos to create slide shows! Click the album you want to display in the sidebar, click the Create button on the Photos toolbar (which bears a plus sign), and then choose Slideshow. Click in the

Slideshow Name text box and type a name for the project; then press Return.

Notice that Photos adds a Slideshows item in the sidebar. A scrolling thumbnail strip appears at the bottom of the Viewer, displaying the images in the album. Click and drag the thumbnails so that they appear in the desired order (see **Figure 10-5**).

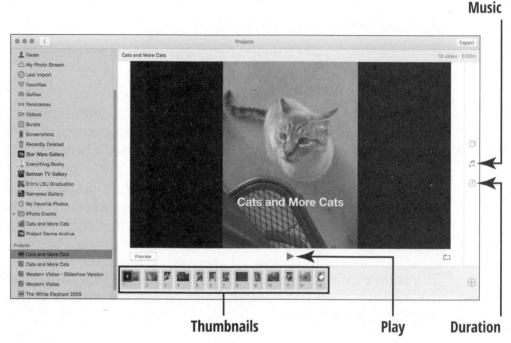

FIGURE 10-5

To choose background music for your slide show, click the Music button at the right side of the window. To choose an Apple theme, click the title to select that perfect song. To choose an iTunes song, display the tracks from your iTunes library by clicking the down arrow next to the Music Library heading; then click the desired songs. The songs you choose appear in the Selected Music list, where you can rearrange them by clicking and dragging. To delete a song from the Selected Music list, hover your cursor over the song entry, and click the circular black button with the X icon.

TIP

To configure the timing for your slide show, click the Duration button at the right side of the window; then click the desired slide in the thumbnail strip. You can specify the amount of time that the slide remains on the screen, as well as set a transition between slides.

When you're ready to play your slide show, click the Play button under the Viewer, and Photos switches to Full Screen mode. You can share your completed slide show as a movie by clicking Export in the upper-right corner of the window.

Edit Photos with Panache

The first step in any editing job is selecting the image you want to fix in the Viewer, which is the default pane in Photos. Then click the Edit button on the Photos toolbar (as shown in the upper-right corner of the window in Figure 10-1) to display the Edit pane controls on the right side of the window, as shown in **Figure 10-6.** Now you're ready to fix problems, using the tools that I discuss in the rest of this section.

Edit your photos with these buttons.

FIGURE 10-6

Change orientation. If an image is in the wrong orientation and needs to be turned to display correctly, click the Rotate button to turn it once counterclockwise. Hold down the Option key while you click the Rotate button to rotate the image clockwise.

Crop photos. Does that photo have an intruder hovering around the edges of the subject? You can remove some of the border by *cropping* an image, just as folks once did with film prints and a pair of scissors. (We've come a long way.) With Photos, you can remove unwanted portions from the edges of an image — a helpful way to remove Uncle Milton's stray head (complete with toupee) from an otherwise-perfect holiday snapshot.

Follow these steps to crop an image:

1. Click the Crop button on the Edit toolbar.

2. Select the portion of the image that you want to keep.

In the Viewer, click and drag the corner handles on the crop square to outline the part of the image you want. Remember that whatever is outside this rectangle disappears when the crop is complete.

TIP

When you drag a corner or edge of the crop square, a semi-opaque grid (familiar to amateur and professional photographers as the nine rectangles from the Rule of Thirds) appears to help you visualize what you're claiming. If you haven't heard of the Rule of Thirds, don't worry: Just try to keep the subject of your photos aligned at one of the grid intersections or running along one of the lines.

3. (Optional) Choose a preset aspect ratio.

If you want to force your cropped selection to a specific size — such as 4" x 3" or 16" x 9" — click the Aspect icon and choose that size from the pop-up menu.

4. Click the Done button.

Oh, and don't forget that you can use the Photos Undo feature (just press ⌘+Z) if you mess up and need to try again.

TIP

Photos features multiple Undo levels, so you can press ⌘+Z several times to travel back through your last several changes. Alternatively, you can always return the image to its original form (before you did any editing at all) by clicking the Revert to Original button.

Improve the image. If a photo looks washed out, click the Enhance button to increase (or decrease) the color saturation and improve the contrast. Enhance is automatic, so you don't have to set anything, but rest assured that you can use Undo if you're not satisfied with the changes.

Fix red-eye. Unfortunately, today's digital cameras can still produce the same "zombies with red eyeballs" as traditional film cameras. *Red-eye* is caused by a camera's flash reflecting off the retinas of a subject's eyes, and it can occur with both humans and pets. Photos can remove that red-eye, however, and turn frightening zombies back into your family and friends! Just click the Red-Eye button and then select a demonized eyeball by clicking the center of it. (If the circular Red-Eye cursor is too small or too large, drag the Size slider to adjust the dimensions.) To complete the process, click the Done button.

IS THAT FACEBOOK, TWITTER, AND FLICKR I SPY?

Indeed it is! Photos provides a direct connection to your Facebook and Twitter social networking accounts and to your Flickr online gallery account, allowing you to simply select one or more photos and send them automatically to the desired service! Click the Share button on the toolbar (refer to Figure 10-1) to select the type of account.

The first time you select photos in the Viewer (or an album in the sidebar) and choose one of these options, Photos prompts you for permission to set up your connection. (Of course, this setup requires you to enter your Facebook, Twitter, and Flickr account information — hence, the confirmation request.) Click Set Up and provide the data that each site requires.

After you set up your accounts, simply select your photos, albums, or events; click the Share toolbar button; and then choose the menu item for the desired service.

Add Photos to Your Email

If you need to send a photo or two of your new car to your relatives, Photos can help you send your images by email by automating the process. The application can prepare your image and embed it automatically in a new message.

To send an image through email, select the image, click the Share button on the toolbar, and then click the Mail menu item. The layout shown in **Figure 10-7** appears. You can also choose the size of the images from the Image Size pop-up menu, which can save considerable downloading time for those recipients who are still using a dial-up connection.

FIGURE 10-7

TIP

Keep in mind that most ISP (Internet service provider) email servers don't accept email messages larger than 10MB, so watch that Size display under the From field. (In fact, the encoding necessary to send images as attachments can *double* the size of each image!) If you're trying to send several images and the total size of the images exceeds 5MB, you may have to click the Image Size pop-up menu and choose a smaller size (reducing the image resolution and size of the file) to embed them all in a single message.

When you're satisfied with the total file size, and you're ready to create your message, type the recipient's email address in the To field (or click the Add button on the right, which bears a plus sign, to select recipients from your Contacts list). Click in the Subject box to enter a subject for the message. When all is ready, click the Send button (the one with a paper-airplane icon) at the top of the window, and Photos sends the message on its way.

Chapter 11

Enjoying Music, Video, and Podcasts

Whether you like classical, jazz, rock, rhythm and blues, folk, or country, I can guarantee you that you won't find a better application than iTunes to fill your life with your music, spoken audio, and video. iTunes — the versatile audio and video player application that comes with your Mac — helps you manage music and other media so it's easy to play, easy to search, and easy to organize.

You can use iTunes on your Mac to

» Play all sorts of digital media, including music, audiobooks, video, TV shows, podcasts (audio journals), and Internet radio.

» Record *(burn)* music to your own custom audio CDs that you can play in your car and home stereo.

» Transfer *(rip)* music from an audio CD to your iTunes library.

» Buy music and video from the iTunes Store — everything from classic jazz to the latest music videos.

» Organize your music into playlists.

Set Up Speakers

If you want to listen to music or other audio files from your Mac, speakers are a must. A typical set of computer stereo speakers will set you back anywhere from $20 to $80, depending on their output. (I prefer speakers that run on AC power rather than battery-operated speakers.) If you're using a MacBook laptop or an iMac, you probably already know that your computer has built-in speakers. You can add external speakers to any Mac in a flash, however. Just make sure that you have AC power handy — another good reason to invest in a surge suppressor strip that provides more outlets. Then follow these steps:

1. Connect the speakers to the computer.

- *USB:* Easy. Just plug the USB cable into any open USB port on your Mac. For more information on connecting USB cables, check out Chapter 2.

digital

- *Traditional audio-jack plug:* Just as easy. Connect the audio cable from the speakers (shown in **Figure 11-1**) to the Headphone or Line Out audio jack on your computer.

2. Plug the speakers into a wall outlet or power strip (if necessary), and turn them on.

FIGURE 11-1

 3. Click the System Preferences icon on the Dock. The System Preferences window appears.

4. Click the Sound icon in the System Preferences window and then click the Output tab, as shown in **Figure 11-2**.

Sound output list

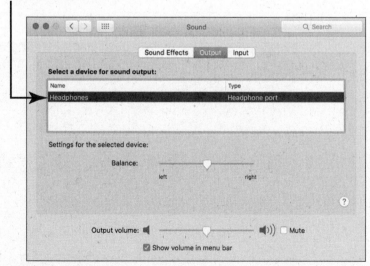

FIGURE 11-2

5. Click the Line Out, Headphones, or USB item in the Sound Output list (depending on the type of speakers you have).

TIP

Did you notice that you can adjust the balance of your speakers from the Sound pane? If one of your speakers is significantly farther away from the computer than the other, use the Balance slider to bring that stereo separation back to normal.

6. Click the Close button in the upper-left corner of the System Preferences window to close the window and save your changes.

Control the Volume

In iTunes, you can control the volume by clicking and dragging the Volume slider, as shown in **Figure 11-3**:

» **To lower the volume,** drag to the left.

» **To raise the volume,** drag to the right.

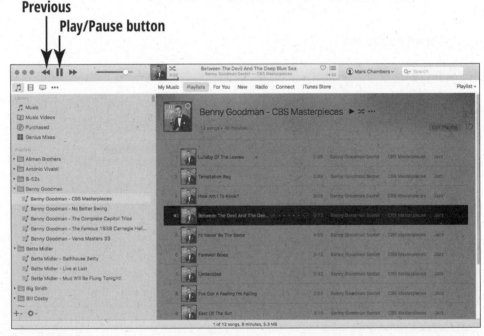

FIGURE 11-3

Does your speaker volume still sound low even after you raise the volume all the way? Don't forget that your Mac has a master volume control that affects all your applications. To change the master volume for your system as a whole, click the Volume icon (looks like a speaker) on the Finder menu bar, and drag the slider up or down. Because this setting affects all applications, if you change the volume on your system, the volume of the selections you hear in iTunes changes as well. (If you're using external speakers, don't forget that they probably have a separate volume control as well.)

TIP

Your Mac keyboard also has dedicated Volume Up and Volume Down keys, as well as a Mute key, so check whether you accidentally pressed the Mute key. Don't forget to check the volume control on your speakers as well!

Add Music from a CD to iTunes

If your Mac has a built-in or external DVD drive, you can easily *rip* (copy) music from an audio CD to iTunes. When you rip a song, you create a copy of the song as a digital music file on your Mac, and songs you save in iTunes reside in its Music Library. To add music to iTunes, follow these steps:

1. Launch iTunes by clicking its icon on the Dock.

2. Load an audio CD into your Mac's DVD drive. If you have an active Internet connection, the CD title is displayed at the top of the window, and the CD track listing appears in the window, as shown in **Figure 11-4**.

3. Decide whether to import all the songs (tracks) on the CD or just the ones you want.

   • *The whole enchilada:* If iTunes asks whether you want to import the contents of the CD into the Music Library, click Yes, and skip the rest of these steps.

   • *Bits and pieces:* If you disabled this prompt by selecting the Don't Show This Again check box, continue with the remaining steps.

CD title   **Import CD button**

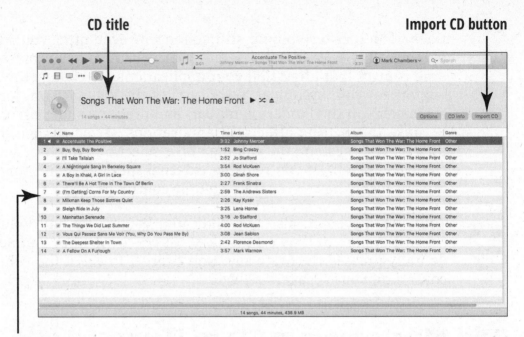

CD tracks

FIGURE 11-4

4. Clear the check box of any song that you don't want to import from the CD. All songs on the CD have a check box next to their titles by default. Unmarked songs aren't imported.

5. Click the Import CD button. iTunes displays a progress bar showing you how many songs remain to import. How long importing takes depends on the length of the songs and the bit rate you're using, but it shouldn't take any longer than two minutes per track. (The default bit rate is the best compromise between audio quality and file size, but you can use a higher bit rate for playback on audiophile stereo equipment.) The songs you've imported appear in your Music Library, and you can click the Music category icon to see all your songs. (More on category icons in a second.)

TIP

iTunes can display your Music Library in several ways. Click the Music icon in the upper-left corner of the window (the one with the musical note); then click on the Playlist drop-down menu at the upper right of the iTunes window (see **Figure 11-5**), and choose the view mode. You can choose to view your Music Library by playlists, songs, albums, artists, composers, or genres.

FIGURE 11-5

Play an Audio CD in iTunes

If your Mac has an internal or external DVD drive, you can play audio CDs with aplomb. Follow these steps:

1. Load the CD into your Mac's drive. By default, iTunes launches automatically, but you can also click the iTunes icon on the Dock to launch it manually.

2. Click the Play/Pause button (refer to Figure 11-3).

TIP

The buttons in iTunes are just like those on a regular CD player. Click the Next button to advance to the next song, and click Previous to return to the beginning of a song. To pause the music, click the Play button, and click it again to restart the music.

Play Digital Music, Video, and Podcasts in iTunes

To play digital files that you added to iTunes from a CD or bought at the iTunes Store (as explained later in this chapter), follow these steps, starting with iTunes open:

1. Click the icon for the media category you want to play. (These icons appear on the left side of the window.) Your choices include Music, Movies, TV Shows, Audiobooks, Internet Radio, and Podcasts. Clicking a category displays media that you downloaded from the iTunes Store or otherwise added to iTunes. Then the selections appear in the track list on the right.

   When you download other types of media from the iTunes Store — such as lectures from iTunes U or apps for an iPhone or iPad — those items appear in the icon list as well. (If you have more categories than iTunes has room to display, click the ellipsis icon, which carries three dots, to display the rest of the categories. See what I mean in Figure 11-4.)

TIP

   Think of a *podcast* as a "spoken magazine," complete with photos and video, ranging over all sorts of topics. Apple offers a wealth of podcasts through the iTunes Store, and virtually all are free of charge.

2. Double-click a specific item to play it or (if you're working with TV shows or podcasts) to display individual episodes. You can also play an entire group of songs, which is called a *playlist* in iTunes-speak. Speaking of playlists. . .

Create and Use an iTunes Playlist

A *playlist* is a specific collection of grouped songs or other media, and you can create them in iTunes. Say you love the song "White Christmas" and have recordings of 20 different artists singing it — and you want a comprehensive playlist of all those songs. You can make a playlist just for them. Playlists are also useful for listening to an entire album or creating the musical background for your next party or road trip. And when you're ready to burn your own CDs (more on that in a bit), starting with an existing playlist is very helpful.

The best way to familiarize yourself with playlists is to create one. Here's how, with iTunes open:

1. Choose File ⇨ New Playlist to begin a new, empty playlist, cleverly named *playlist*.

TIP

    You can also click the Create button (a plus-sign icon) in the bottom-left corner of the iTunes window and choose New Playlist from the pop-up menu.

2. Give the playlist a name. The new playlist is already highlighted, so go right ahead and type a new name. Then press Return to save the name. (You'll notice that the new playlist now appears in the Playlists section of the iTunes sidebar on the left side of the window.)

TIP

    If the sidebar doesn't appear in your iTunes window, just click the Playlists button in the center of the iTunes toolbar.

3. Add a *track* (another term for a song) from the Music Library to your new playlist:

    a. *Click the Music entry in the sidebar on the left, or click the Music category icon.*

    b. *Find the song you want to include from the track list on the right, and drag it to your new playlist entry in the sidebar.* That's it! The playlist now contains your song.

4. Repeat Step 3b to add as many tracks as you like to the playlist. You can select multiple tracks to drag by holding down the Command (⌘) key while you click.

When your playlist is complete, you're ready to play your songs in iTunes. Simply click the desired playlist in the sidebar to display the songs and then double-click the first song in the playlist.

When you're familiar with a basic playlist, check out these playlist tips:

» **Pick tracks first.** You may find it easier to select the songs you want for a playlist and then create a new playlist for them automatically. Select the desired tracks from the track list by holding down the ⌘ key while you click; then choose File ⇨ New ⇨ New Playlist from Selection. This action creates a new playlist and automatically adds any tracks selected in the Music Library. iTunes also attempts to name the playlist automatically for you.

» **Rename a playlist.** Click the playlist name in the sidebar to select it, wait a second, and then click the name again. A text box opens, allowing you to type the new playlist name.

» **Reorder tracks.** Display the playlist; then click and drag any track to the desired order within the track list.

» **Reuse tracks.** You can add the same song to any number of playlists because the songs in a playlist are simply pointers to songs in your Music Library — not to the songs themselves. Add them to, and remove them from, any playlist at will, secure in the knowledge that the songs remain safe in the library.

» **Delete tracks.** To delete a track from a playlist, select the playlist to display the tracks, click the offending track to select it, and then press Delete.

» **Delete playlists.** As for removing playlists themselves, that's simple, too. Just select the playlist in the source list and press Delete.

Burn an Audio CD in iTunes

Besides being a fantastic audio player, iTunes is adept at creating CDs. iTunes makes copying songs to a CD as simple as a few clicks. Your Mac needs either a built-in DVD drive or an external USB DVD recorder to work this magic.

TIP

It's easy to prepare for audio CD burning! Pick up a pack of standard blank audio CDs (sometimes called "music CDs"), which are rated at 700MB and 80 minutes (storage capacity). Don't forget a permanent marker to label your new discs (write on the top side), or if you're feeling fancy, consider using printed labels. Finally, don't forget to buy a pack of empty CD sleeves or hinged plastic jewel cases if you need them.

It's easier to burn a CD from an existing playlist, so see the earlier section on how to do that, and build your burn playlist first. Then follow these steps, with iTunes open:

1. Click the existing playlist that you want to copy. Remember that your audio CD can store only about 80 minutes of audio, which is about 20 songs of 4 minutes each.

TIP

iTunes also warns you if the amount of audio you're trying to record exceeds the capacity of the disc.

2. Choose File ➪ Burn Playlist to Disc.

3. In the Burn Settings dialog that appears, choose Maximum Possible from the Preferred Speed menu. Then select the Audio CD disc format radio button, as shown in **Figure 11-6**.

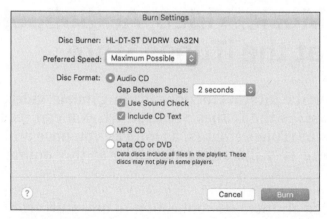

FIGURE 11-6

4. Click the Burn button to commence the disc burning process.

5. Put the blank CD in the drive when iTunes prompts you to load it. iTunes starts the process, which will probably take about 5 minutes, and lets you know when the recording is complete — on some Macs, iTunes ejects your new disc automatically, whereas on other models you may have to right-click on the Audio CD entry in the sidebar and choose Eject from the pop-up menu.

Watch Visualizations

iTunes is indeed a feast for the ears, and it can provide eye candy as well. With just a click or two, you can view mind–bending graphics that stretch, move, and pulse with your music. Follow these steps:

1. Double-click a favorite song or playlist to play it.

2. Choose View ⇨ Show Visualizer (or press ⌘+T). iTunes automatically enters full-screen mode, allowing you the best display of those mind-bending animations.

3. To escape from Full Screen mode and stop the visual display, press Esc.

Find and Buy Music, Video, Audiobooks, and Podcasts at the iTunes Store

The hottest spot on the Internet for downloading music, video, audio-books, and podcasts is the iTunes Store, which you can reach from the cozy confines of iTunes (that is, as long as you have an Internet connection). **Figure 11-7** illustrates the lobby of this online audio–video store.

TIP

Naturally, you need an Internet connection to buy stuff from the iTunes Store and listen to Internet radio. If you're not connected yet, visit Chapter 13 to find more about joining the Internet crowd.

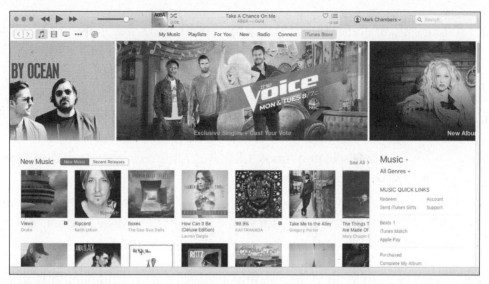

FIGURE 11-7

You can search for a specific item (or browse to your heart's content) within the iTunes Store by following these steps:

1. Click the iTunes Store button on the iTunes toolbar. After a few moments, you see the home screen, which features the latest offerings.

2. Browse the items in the store or search for an item:

- Click a link in the Store list to browse according to media type.

- Click a featured artist or album thumbnail to jump directly to the page for that artist or album.

- Click in the Search box in the top-right corner and type an album or artist name.

- Click the Genres link at the top of the list on the right side of the window to search by musical genre.

TIP

To display the details of a specific album, song, or audiobook, just click it. iTunes allows you to preview a 90-second sample of any audio or video for free; just double-click the entry or click the Preview button for movies and music videos.

3. Add an item you want to your iTunes Store shopping cart by clicking the Buy Song/Movie/Album/Video button. (The name of the button changes depending on the type of media you want to buy.)

   - *Individual tracks:* If you're interested in buying just certain tracks (for that perfect road-warrior mix), you would add just that song (or those songs).

   - *A whole album or book:* Click Buy Album or, to buy an audiobook, click the Buy Book button.

4. Enter your Apple ID and password when iTunes prompts you for them. (For more on your Apple ID, see the nearby sidebar "Set up an Apple ID.")

TIP

You can download individual episodes of a podcast, but you can also *subscribe* to a podcast. When you subscribe, iTunes automatically downloads future episodes and adds them to the Podcasts item in your source list.

SET UP AN APPLE ID

Time to back up a sec. You need an Apple ID (also called an *iCloud password* within OS X) to buy something from the iTunes Store. This ID is how Apple securely stores your payment method, email address, and contact information so that you can purchase things easily, without having to reenter all that stuff every time you buy an album or a movie. Also, Apple can use the Apple ID you created while using the Setup Assistant in Chapter 2 — less hassle, less confusion. If you set up your Mac *without* creating an Apple ID/iCloud password, just click the Create Apple ID button when prompted.

Depending on what you've already set up, just click the Buy button, and iTunes leads you step by step through the account setup process (or whisks you right to the payment process). Remember that all the information you send goes over an encrypted connection. Way to go, Apple.

Some songs (and most podcasts) are free to download. Apple always clearly indicates whether a download is free, and you get a receipt in an email for every purchase . . . yet another reason to have an Apple ID account!

After you buy an item, it automatically begins downloading. The items you download are then saved to the separate Purchased playlist (under the Library heading in the sidebar). From there, you can play them or move them to other playlists just like any other items in your iTunes library.

Although the stuff you buy remains in the Purchased category in the source list, each item is automatically moved to the proper category as well. Any songs you buy are added automatically to the Music category in the sidebar, for example; any movies you buy are added to the Movies category, and TV shows go in the TV category.

TIP

The Back and Forward buttons in the top-left corner of the iTunes Store window operate much like those in the Safari web browser (see Chapter 14), moving you backward or forward in sequence through pages you've already seen.

Chapter 12

Playing Games in El Capitan

lthough OS X comes with at least one game — an excellent version of chess — the Mac has never been considered a serious gaming platform by most computer owners. Until recently, many popular Windows games were never released in versions for the Mac, and only the most expensive Mac models had a first-rate 3D video card.

However, all of today's Mac models feature muscle car–quality video cards that can handle most complex 3D graphics with ease. Match that capability with the renewed popularity of the Mac as a home computer and the performance of the current crop of Intel-based processors, and your Mac is quite the game machine.

In this chapter, you

» Play 3D chess with your Mac.

» Burn a little time with an old-fashioned sliding tile puzzle.

» Download new games for your Dashboard widget collection.

» Download new games (and other software) for your Mac from the App Store.

» Find out more about online gaming.

Play Chess

Chess has no flashy weapons and no cities to raze, but it's still the world's most popular game, and the OS X version even includes 3D pizzazz. **Figure 12-1** illustrates the Chess application at play; you can find it in your Applications folder.

Click and drag a piece to move it.

FIGURE 12-1

As you might expect, moving pieces on this board is as simple as clicking a piece and dragging it to its (legal) ending position.

The game features take-back (or undo) for your last move; just press ⌘+Z if you need a second chance. You can save games in progress from the Game menu and even display your game log in text form from the Moves menu. Maybe Chess doesn't have the complete set of bells and whistles that commercial chess games have, but the price is right, and the play can be quite challenging (and the moves take much longer to calculate) when you set it at the higher skill levels.

To configure Chess to your liking, choose Chess ⇨ Preferences. Then you can

» **Change the appearance of your board and pieces.** Try a set of fur pieces on a grass board — jungle chess at its best!

» **Turn on spoken moves and voice recognition.** Click to select the Speak Computer Moves check box and then click the Computer Voice pop-up menu to select the voice your Mac uses.

» **Set the computer's skill level.** The Faster/Stronger slider determines whether your Mac plays a faster or smarter game.

TIP

If you're like me, a hint at midgame isn't really cheating — especially when I'm behind by several pieces! When it's your turn, choose Moves ⇨ Show Hint and watch Chess suggest the best move.

Play the Tile Game Widget

Apple also provides a digital version of that old standby, the sliding tile game. Tile Game is a Dashboard widget, so you can display it at any time by pressing the correct function key (F4 or F12, depending on the keyboard your Mac uses).

If you're using a trackpad, display Mission Control (by swiping upward with three fingers) and click the Dashboard thumbnail.

Figure 12-2 illustrates the Tile Game widget on my Dashboard.

Tile Game widget

FIGURE 12-2

TIP

If the Tile Game widget doesn't appear on your Dashboard, click the Add button (bearing the plus-sign icon) at the lower left to display your available widgets. Click the Tile Game icon, and El Capitan adds it to your Dashboard.

Click the Tile Game window once to randomize the tiles and then click again to start playing. To move a tile to the free space, click the tile. The object of the game, of course, is to restore the image to its original pristine condition!

You can return to your applications and your El Capitan Desktop at any time by pressing the Esc key again or by pressing the Dashboard function key again.

TIP

One nice thing about Dashboard game widgets is that most of them save the current game (or position) when you close the Dashboard. That way, you can easily resume the game after you . . . well, get real work done.

Find more information about displaying and configuring widgets in Chapter 3.

Install New Widget Games from Apple

Looking for a new gaming challenge for your Dashboard? No problem. Apple offers additional game widgets that you can download from Apple. Third-party software developers also provide both freeware and shareware widget games. When the download is complete, El Capitan automatically prompts you for confirmation before installing the new widget.

To download a new game and add it to your Dashboard, follow these steps:

1. Display your Dashboard by pressing the Dashboard function key.

2. Click the Add button (which bears a plus sign, naturally) in the lower-left corner of the Dashboard screen; then click the More Widgets button that appears. El Capitan opens the Widget Download screen, using your Safari web browser, as shown in **Figure 12-3**.

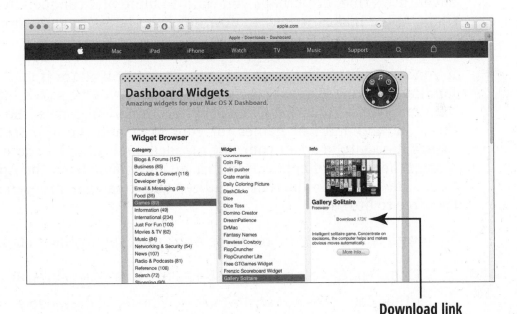

Download link

FIGURE 12-3

3. Browse the different widget categories until you've located a widget you'd like to add to your Dashboard.

4. Click the Download link. The Widget Installer prompts you for confirmation before the widget is added to your available widgets.

5. Click the new icon in the list of available widgets. El Capitan adds it to your Dashboard screen.

Don't forget to set any options that your new game offers; look for a tiny circle with a lowercase letter *i*. Click this information icon, and you can set the options that are available for the game.

Download New Games from Apple

Widget games are somewhat limited, of course. Maybe you'd like to try a cutting-edge first-person shooting game or a sophisticated adventure game, or perhaps you want to build and conquer civilizations. Apple makes it easy to download the latest in game applications from the App Store.

If you've used the App Store on your iPhone or iPad (or if you're familiar with the iTunes Store within iTunes), you've sailed into familiar waters. You can download both commercial games (those that you buy) and free games for your Mac, and the App Store makes it easy to keep all your downloaded applications updated. Many other types of applications are also available from the App Store, including productivity, utility, and financial programs. Feel free to browse!

To download a new game from the App Store, follow these steps:

1. Click the App Store button on the Dock (it's a blue circle with an *A*).

2. Click the Categories icon on the toolbar at the top of the window and then click Games. You should see selections like those shown in **Figure 12-4**.

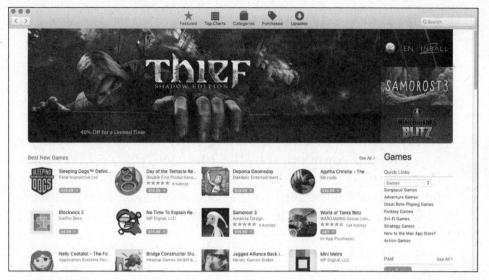

FIGURE 12-4

3. Click a game to display information about the game, such as the age rating, the size of the game, and representative screen shots.

4. To download the game, click the price button in the top-left corner of the App Store window.

TIP

Many games are free, and they display a button marked *Free*.

The button changes to read either Buy App (for a purchase) or Install App.

5. Click the button again to continue.

The App Store prompts you for your Apple ID and password.

6. Enter your Apple ID and password, and then click the Sign In button. The game begins to download.

TIP

If you didn't create an Apple ID (also called an iCloud account) during El Capitan setup — or if you don't already have one for use with your iPhone, iPod touch, or iPad — click the Create Apple ID button. The App Store leads you through the process.

When the download is complete, the game appears in Launchpad, ready for you to play.

Play Games Online

Some of today's hottest games aren't limited to your Mac. Online games use your Internet connection to match you against thousands of other players, in real time, across the world!

TIP

In my opinion, online gaming is truly enjoyable only if you have a broadband connection to the Internet (DSL, cable, or satellite). Playing today's 3D online games (or even web-based games) by using a dial-up modem connection is a lesson in frustration. Turn to Chapter 13 if you still need to choose an Internet connection.

Some games are free and display advertisements, and others are subscription-based.

Probably the most popular online game for the Mac is the online megahit *World of Warcraft*. This massive multiplayer online role-playing game, or MMORPG, is another wrinkle in the popular *Warcraft* game series. *World of Warcraft* puts the character you create in the boots of human princes, Orc battle generals, undead champions, trolls, gnomes, and elfin lords. In fact, you can create multiple characters and play them as you choose. For all the details, check the official site at www.blizzard.com.

If more traditional games such as bridge and sudoku are your preference, I heartily recommend the CNN Games page (http://games.cnn.com). You can choose among a wide range of free online games, including arcade, strategy, word, and card games. (Most even include snappy music while you play!) Leaderboards keep track of your high scores, naturally, and you can play solo or against your friends online.

TIP

One word of caution while playing games online: *Never* provide any private information other than your name and your email address while signing up for a free game. (This includes, of course, your credit card or PayPal account information unless you're signing up for a commercial online game that requires a subscription.) Games provided by high-quality websites such as CNN certainly aren't scams, of course, but it pays to be careful. I always recommend avoiding online games that overwhelm you with advertisements, or so-called "free" games that require you to download something to play!

4

Exploring the Internet

Chapter 13

Understanding Internet Basics

The Internet is a terribly complex monster of a network. If you tried to fathom all the data that's exchanged on the Internet and everything that takes place when you check your email for your cousin Joan's fruitcake recipe, your brain would probably melt like a chocolate bar in the Sahara Desert.

Luckily for regular folks like you and me, OS X El Capitan closes the trapdoor on all these details, keeping them hidden (as they *should* be). You don't have to worry about them, and the obscure information you need to establish an Internet connection is kept to a minimum. You need to know only the basics about the Internet to actually use and enjoy the Internet, and that's what I provide in this chapter!

I discuss how to

» Use different types of Internet connections.

» Connect to the Internet.

» Join Apple's iCloud service.

» Add an antivirus program.

» Follow common-sense rules to stay safe on the Internet.

Understand How the Internet Works

Many computer owners I talk to are convinced that the Internet is a real object. They're not quite sure whether it's animal, vegetable, or mineral, but they're sure that they either *have it* or *want it* inside their computers. (It's probably a tiny, glowing ball: a cross between Tinker Bell and St. Elmo's fire.)

Seriously, though, you don't need to know what the Internet is to use it. From a Mac owner's standpoint, you would be correct (in a way) if you said that the Internet begins at the DSL connection or the cable modem. Therefore, if you want to skip to the next section and avoid a glance underneath the hood, be my guest.

Still here? Good. Here's a brief description of what happens when you connect to the Internet and visit a website:

1. You open your Safari web browser (a *browser* is a program used to display pages from the World Wide Web), and your Mac connects to an Internet service provider (ISP) or a public Internet access point. From the moment your Mac connects, you're officially online and part of the Internet. (Note, however, that you're not on the web yet — just connected to the Internet.)

An *ISP* is simply the company you pay to connect to the Internet. You might contract with a cable company (such as Comcast or Mediacom) or a phone company (like AT&T), or you might use a service such as AOL. All these are ISPs. Your ISP account usually includes reserved space on its computers for you to create a personal website, as well as giving you one, two, or more email addresses.

2. Your ISP locates the website across the Internet.

When you ask to open a specific website, your ISP uses that website's name to locate the computer it resides on. In the Internet world, the website *name* is its web address, or URL (which stands for *Universal Resource Locator,* but you don't need to remember that). When the website is located, your ISP opens a sort of pathway between your Mac and the server that website resides on. If you request the URL www.mlcbooks.com, for example, my business website is displayed.

3. After you connect to a website, a web page is displayed. On this page, you can click *links,* which generally consist of text shown in a different color, and the text is often underlined. Sometimes, however, the link is an image rather than text. Clicking the text or image link opens another page on the same website, or it may even open a different website.

This is the essence of everything you do on the Internet: Computers connect with other computers (no matter where on the planet they may be) and exchange information of various types, such as email messages, photos, web pages, videos, and music.

See? It's beautifully organized chaos, and you can visit any of the billions of websites on the planet from the comfort of your keyboard!

Explore Internet Connections

Consider the types of connections that are available under El Capitan to link your Mac to your ISP (see the preceding section). You can choose any of four pathways to digital freedom:

» **A broadband connection:** Whether it's by way of DSL (which uses a standard telephone line) or cable (which uses your cable

TV wiring), broadband Internet access is many times faster than old-fashioned dial-up connections. Also, DSL and cable technologies are *always-on:* that is, your computer is automatically connected to the Internet when you turn it on, and the connection stays active. With DSL or cable, no squeaky-squawky cacophony occurs when your modem makes a connection each time you want to check your movie-listings website. Both DSL and cable require a special piece of hardware, commonly called a *modem.* This box is usually rented to you as part of your ISP charge. A broadband connection usually requires professional installation.

TIP

Not every Internet connection requires an ISP. Some mobile phone providers can equip your laptop with a cellular modem that delivers the Internet wherever you have mobile service. Some mobile phone providers can also turn your smartphone into a wireless Internet hotspot. And nowadays, some larger cities now offer free citywide public wireless (Wi-Fi) access (not to mention the free wireless access you can often find provided by coffee shops, restaurants, and hotels).

» **A satellite connection:** If you're *really* out there — miles and miles away from any cable or DSL phone service — you can still have high-speed Internet access. The price of a satellite connection is usually much steeper than that of a standard DSL or cable connection, but it's available anywhere you can plant your antenna dish with a clear view of the sky.

» **A dial-up connection:** Old-fashioned, yes. Slow as an arthritic burro, indeed. However, an *analog* (or telephone modem) connection is still a viable method for computer owners to reach the Internet. It's the least-expensive method available (as long as your call to the access number is a local call and not a long-distance, toll charge), and all you need for this type of connection are a standard telephone jack, an analog modem, and a contract with a service provider (such as AOL). Apple used to include a modem with every computer, but no longer. These days, you have to buy an external USB modem to make the dial-up connection. (Any USB modem that's compatible with OS X El Capitan works fine.)

TIP

I'll be honest, dear reader: If you have access to *any* other method of connecting to the Internet, give dial-up access a wide berth. A dial-up connection is simply too slow by today's standards.

» **A network connection:** This type of connection concerns Mac models that are part of a local area network (LAN) either at the office or in your home. (A *network* simply means a community of computers that can talk to one another and share files and devices, such as a printer.) If your Mac is connected to a LAN that already has Internet access, you don't even need an ISP, and no other hardware is required: Simply contact your network administrator, buy that important person a steak dinner, and ask to be connected to the Internet. On the other hand, if your network has no Internet access, you're back to Square One: You need one of the three types of connections noted in the preceding bullets.

Set Up a Broadband Internet Connection

Okay, so you sign up for Internet access, and your ISP sends you a sheet of paper covered with indecipherable settings that look like Egyptian hieroglyphics. Don't worry: Those settings are the ones you need to connect to your ISP. After you transfer this information to El Capitan, you should be surfing the web like an old pro. (First, of course, you need to connect your Mac to the DSL or cable modem, as instructed by your ISP.)

Follow these steps to set up your Internet connection if you're using a cable modem, DSL connection, or network:

1. Click the System Preferences icon on the Dock, and click the Network icon.

2. Select Ethernet in the list on the left side of the pane to display the settings you see in **Figure 13-1**.

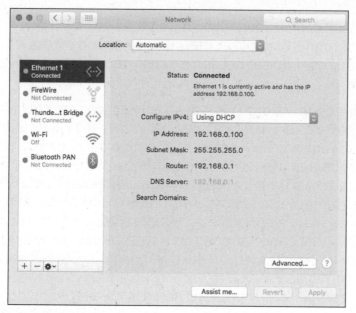

FIGURE 13-1

3. Refer to the paperwork or email you received from your ISP and then enter the settings for the type of connection your ISP offers:

- *If your ISP tells you to use Dynamic Host Configuration Protocol (DHCP):* Choose Using DHCP from the Configure IPv4 pop-up menu, and your ISP can automatically set up virtually all the connection settings for you! (No wonder DHCP is so popular these days.)

- *If your ISP tells you that you won't use DHCP:* Choose Manually from the Configure IPv4 pop-up menu. Then enter the settings provided by your ISP in the IP Address, Subnet Mask, Router, and DNS Server fields.

4. If your ISP uses PPPoE (Point-to-Point Protocol over Ethernet), choose Create PPPoE Service from the Configure IPv4 pop-up menu. (If your ISP doesn't use PPPoE, skip to Step 8.)

5. Type an identifying name for the PPPoE service (such as the name of your ISP) in the Service Name text box.

6. Click Done to display the PPPoE connection settings.

7. Enter the password for your PPPoE connection, as provided by your ISP, and then click Apply. (This is yet another good reason to store all the connection setup data from your ISP in a safe place.)

8. Press ⌘+Q to close System Preferences and save your changes.

 El Capitan can get down and dirty in the configuration trenches! To launch an assistant to help with the configuration process, click the Assist Me button at the bottom of the System Preferences Network pane, and then click Assistant on the assistant's welcome screen.

Set Up a Wireless Internet Connection

If you're within range of a wireless Ethernet network, you can use your Mac's built-in wireless hardware to connect. (*Ethernet* is the networking type used by most homes and businesses, and it can be either a wired or wireless connection.) Most public networks offer Internet access, so this option is an advantage for MacBook owners on the go (those who visit coffee shops, libraries, and schools, for example).

Likewise, if you're using a broadband connection at home with an AirPort Extreme wireless router or Time Capsule wireless backup device, your desktop Mac can connect to that wireless network and reach the Internet that way.

Follow these steps to connect to a wireless network:

1. Click the System Preferences icon on the Dock.

2. Click the Network icon.

3. From the Connection list on the left, choose Wi-Fi.

4. Select the Show Wi-Fi Status in Menu Bar check box.

5. Click the Apply button.

6. Press ⌘+Q to close System Preferences and save your settings.

7. Click the Wi-Fi status icon on the Finder menu bar.

This icon looks just like the wireless status indicator on iPhones and other wireless devices — a fan shape composed of bars that indicate signal strength.

8. From the menu of available Wi-Fi connections that appears, choose an existing network connection that you want to join.

   The network name is usually posted for public networks. If you're joining a private wireless network, ask the person who set up the network for the name you should choose.

9. If you're joining a secure network, El Capitan prompts you for a password, so just enter the password and click Join. If the network is open and unsecured, El Capitan won't prompt you for a password, and the connection is made. (However, you should always be cautious about joining an open network unless you're sure it's safe — typically, because you know the person or organization providing that network.)

TIP

A *secure network* is closed to those without the password, preventing outsiders from connecting to your Mac.

Again, if the public network you're joining has a password (most public networks don't), it should be posted. If you're joining a private wireless network, ask the good person who set up the network for that all-important password.

Set Up a Dial-Up Connection

Follow these steps to set up your Internet connection if you're using a standard phone line and your Mac's external USB modem:

1. Click the System Preferences icon on the Dock, and choose Network.

2. Choose External Modem from the list at the left.

3. Click the TCP/IP tab, and enter the settings for the type of connection your ISP provides:

   • *If your ISP tells you to use PPP (Point-to-Point Protocol):* Choose Using PPP from the Configure IPv4 pop-up menu. If your ISP provided you DNS Server or Search Domain addresses, type them in the corresponding boxes.

- *If you're using AOL:* Choose AOL Dialup from the Configure IPv4 pop-up menu. If AOL provided you DNS Server or Search Domain addresses, click the corresponding box and type them.

- *If your ISP instructs you to set up the connection manually:* Choose Manually from the Configure IPv4 pop-up menu. Then click the IP Address, DNS Server, and Search Domain fields and enter the respective settings provided by your ISP.

4. Click the PPP tab.

5. In their proper fields, enter the account name, password, telephone number, service provider name (optional), and an alternative telephone number provided by your ISP.

6. Press ⌘+Q to close System Preferences and save your changes.

Find Out about iCloud

In ancient times — I'm talking five years ago here — when you took a photo with your iPhone or created a new document with your iPad, your new additions just *sat* there (in their original location) until you had a chance to sync your device with your Mac. Music that you bought from the iTunes Store on your Mac remained on your computer until you synchronized your iPhone, iPad, or iPod touch over your trusty USB cable connection.

Ah, how progress marches on! Now you can share data between your Mac and your iOS devices — your iPhone, iPad, and iPod touch — automatically across a wireless connection! If you buy an album on your Mac these days, it can just *show up* on your iPhone or iPad automatically.

That's Apple's iCloud online service. In this section, I save you the trouble of researching all the benefits of iCloud. Heck, that's one of the reasons you bought this book, right?

Today's Apple iOS devices can all display or play the same media: photos, music, books, TV shows, and such. iOS devices can even share and edit documents from many of the same applications you use on your Mac. Therefore, it makes sense to effortlessly share all your digital media across these devices, and that's what iCloud is all about. Apple calls this synchronization *pushing*.

Take a look at how the pushing process works. Imagine that you just completed a Pages document on your MacBook (an invitation for your grandson's birthday party), but you're traveling on the road, and you need to get the document to your family members so that they can edit and print it with your son's iPad.

Before iCloud, you'd have to attach the document to an email message or upload it to some type of online storage; then a family member would have to download and save the document to the iPad before working with it. With iCloud, you simply save the document, and your MacBook automatically pushes the document to the iPad! Your document appears on the iPad, ready to be opened, edited, and printed (and on any other iOS devices that you've authorized as well). iCloud sets up this push system only between computers and devices that use the same Apple ID, so your data remains private.

iCloud isn't limited to digital media, either. Your Mac can also automatically synchronize your email, iCal calendars, and Address Book contacts with other iOS devices across the Internet, making it much easier to stay in touch no matter which device you happen to be using at the moment.

Apple also throws in 5GB (a lot!) of free online storage that you can use for all sorts of things: not only digital media files but also documents and anything else that you'd like to place online for safekeeping. Even better, anything you buy through the iTunes Store — such as music, video, and applications — doesn't count against your 5GB limit. You can save files and folders on your iCloud Drive, which is available on both your Mac computers and your iOS devices.

Need more elbow room than 5GB? At the time of this writing, Apple is happy to provide 50, 200, or even 1TB of additional storage for a monthly subscription fee of $0.99, $2.99, or $9.99, respectively. Click the Manage button on the iCloud pane in System Preferences and then click Buy More Storage. Remember that to join the iCloud revolution, you need an iCloud account (also called an Apple ID).

You can create one during the El Capitan setup process I describe in Chapter 2, but you're also prompted to create one whenever an iCloud account is necessary. And after you create your iCloud account, you can use it on all your Apple computers and devices.

I should mention that you get a free iCloud email address, which ends in the rather catchy @me.com. You can also send and receive iCloud email seamlessly from El Capitan's Mail program, which is the preferred method of checking messages. In fact, El Capitan automatically creates a matching Mail account for your iCloud email address. Unadulterated *cool!*

You control all iCloud settings from the iCloud pane in System Preferences, as shown in **Figure 13-2**. Click the System Preferences icon on the Dock and then click the iCloud icon. If you're not an iCloud member already, enter your iCloud account and your password, and System Preferences guides you through basic iCloud configuration by asking you questions.

FIGURE 13-2

TIP

To display the particulars about your iCloud storage, click the Manage button in the bottom-right corner of the iCloud Preferences pane. On the sheet that appears, you can see how much space you're using for specific types of documents and applications.

Like the convenient operating system it is, El Capitan handles all your iCloud chores automatically from this point on.

Keep in mind that iCloud is many things, but it isn't an ISP. You need an existing Internet connection to use the features included in iCloud membership. This requirement makes a lot of sense, considering that most of us already have Internet access.

iCloud works with the ISP you already have, so you don't have to worry that AT&T or AOL will conflict with iCloud. However, I can't guarantee that your system administrator at work allows iCloud traffic across his or her pristine network. Perhaps a box of doughnuts would help your argument.

Keep Your Mac Secure Online

I know that you've heard horror stories about hacking: Big corporations and big government installations seem to be as open to hackers as a public library. Often, you read that entire identities are being stolen online. When you consider that your Mac can contain extremely sensitive and private information from your life — such as your Social Security number and financial information — it's enough to make you nervous about turning on your computer long enough to check your eBay auctions.

How much of this is Hollywood-style drama? How truly *real* is the danger, especially to Mac owners? In this section, I continue a quest that I've pursued for almost 20 years: making my readers feel comfortable and secure in the online world by explaining the truth about what can happen and telling you how you can protect your system from intrusions.

TIP

One quick note: This section is written with the home and small-business Mac owner in mind. Macs that access the Internet over a larger corporate network are likely already protected by that knight in shining armor: the network system administrator. (Insert applause here.) Check with your system administrator before you attempt to implement any of the recommendations I make here.

As a consultant, I've run websites and squashed virus attacks for many companies and organizations in my hometown, so I've seen the gamut of Internet dangers. With that understood, here's what can happen to you online *without* the right safeguards, on *any* computer:

» **Hackers can access shared information on your network.** If you're running an unguarded network, it's possible for others to gain access to your documents and applications or wreak havoc on your system.

» **Your system could become infected with a virus or dangerous macro.** Left to their own devices, these misbehaving programs and macro commands can delete files or turn your entire hard drive into an empty paperweight. (Although Mac viruses are few as I write this book, I don't think we'll enjoy such luxury for long.)

» **Unsavory individuals can attempt to contact members of your family.** This type of attack can take place over Messages (the Apple instant-messaging and conferencing program, which I describe in Chapter 16), email, or web discussion boards, putting your family's safety at risk.

» **Hackers can use your system to attack others.** Your computer can be tricked into helping hackers when they attempt to knock out websites on the Internet.

» **Criminals can attempt to con you out of your credit card or personal information.** The Internet is a prime tool used by people trying to steal identities.

To be absolutely honest, just like every time you drive a car, some danger is indeed present every time you or any user of your Mac connects to the Internet. However, here's the good news: If you use the proper safeguards, it's impossible for most of those worst-case scenarios to happen on your Mac, and the rest would be so difficult that even the most diehard hacker would throw in the towel long before reaching your computer or network.

I want to point out that virtually everyone reading this book — as well as the guy writing it — really doesn't have anything that's worth a malicious hacking campaign. Information in the form of Quicken data files, saved games of *Sims 4*, and genealogical data might be priceless to us, of course, but most dedicated hackers are after bigger game. Unfortunately, the coverage that the media and Hollywood give to corporate and government attacks can make even Batman's Aunt Harriet more than a little paranoid. It's not really necessary to consider the FBI or Interpol every time you poke your Mac's power button. A few simple precautions (and a healthy dose of common sense) are all that's required.

TIP

Because this book focuses on OS X El Capitan, I don't spend much time covering Windows. For a comprehensive guide to Windows 10 and the PC world, however, I can heartily recommend *PCs All-in-One For Dummies* (John Wiley & Sons, Inc.). Why the strong recommendation? Well, I wrote that book, too!

TIP

Interested in the technical side of computer security? Visit a favorite site of mine on the web: www.grc.com, the home of Gibson Research Corporation. There you'll find the free online utility ShieldsUP!, which automatically tests how susceptible your Mac is to hacker attacks.

Know the Antivirus Basics

It's time to consider your antivirus protection under both El Capitan and Windows. *Viruses* are malicious computer programs that originate at an outside source and can infect your computer without your knowing it. The virus, which is generally activated when you run an infected program on your computer, can then take control of your system and cause lots of trouble. You need to closely monitor what I call the Big Three:

» **Web downloads:** Consider every file you receive from websites on the Internet to be a possible viral threat, including things like application files and Word documents.

» **Removable media:** Viruses can be stored on everything from CD-ROMs and DVD-ROMs to USB flash drives.

» **Email file attachments:** An application sent to you as an email attachment is an easy doorway to your system. (Yet another reason to follow proper "Netiquette" and avoid sending spurious email attachments. If you forward an email file attachment you received from another person without scanning it, you run the risk of sending an unwelcome stowaway as well!)

Horrors! OS X has no built-in antivirus support. However, a good antivirus program takes care of any application that's carrying a virus. Make sure that the antivirus program you choose offers *real-time scanning,* which operates when you download or open a file. Periodic scanning of your entire system is important, too, but only a real-time scanning application such as VirusBarrier X8 can immediately ensure that the file or the application you just received in your email Inbox is truly free from viruses.

Keep in mind that Apple periodically releases software updates for El Capitan that are intended to plug security holes as the holes are discovered. So if you get into the habit of grabbing these updates whenever they're available, you can help keep your Mac safe. (Chapter 17 covers how to set up automatic updates to El Capitan.)

Virus technology continues to evolve over time, just like more beneficial application development. A recently discovered virus, for example, was contained in a JPEG image file! With a good antivirus application that offers regular updates, you can continue to keep your system safe from viral attack.

I heartily recommend both ClamXav (www.clamxav.com) and the application VirusBarrier X8 from Intego (https://www.intego.com). Both programs include automatic updates delivered while you're online to make sure that you're covered against the latest viruses.

Follow Common Sense: Things Not to Do Online

Practicing common sense on the Internet is just as important as adding an antivirus application to your Mac.

With this statement in mind, here's a checklist of things you should *never* do while you're online:

» **Download a file from a site you don't trust.** Make sure that your antivirus software is configured to check downloaded files before you open them.

» **Open an email attachment before it's checked.** Don't give in to temptation, even if the person who sent the message is someone you trust. (Many macro viruses now replicate themselves by sending copies to the addresses found in the victim's email program. This problem crops up regularly in the Windows world, but it has been known to happen in the Mac community as well.)

TIP

If you're ever in doubt about a file that someone has sent you, write the sender an email and ask whether he sent it! Sometimes, the wording in the Subject line is misspelled or uses wording your friend wouldn't choose. Things like that should raise your eyebrow.

» **Enter personal information in an email message when you don't know the recipient.** Sure, I send my mailing address to friends and family, but no one else.

» **Enter personal information on a website provided as a link in an email message.** Don't fall prey to phishing expeditions. *Phishing* is an Internet term that refers to the attempt that con artists and hackers make to lure you in by creating websites that look just like the sites used by major online stores — including big names such as eBay, PayPal, and Amazon. These turkeys then send junk email messages telling you that you must log on to the website to "refresh" or "correct" your personal information. As you've no doubt already guessed, that information is siphoned off and sold to the highest bidder — *your* credit card number, *your* password, and *your* address. (In fact, if you hover your pointer over the links on a phishing website, you'll notice that they go to Internet addresses different from the ones where they claim to go.) Luckily, if you follow the tips I give you in this section, you can avoid these phishing expeditions.

Some of these email message and website combinations look authentic enough to fool anyone! It's important to remember **that no reputable online company or store will demand or solicit your personal information by using email or a linked website.** In fact, feel free to contact the company at its *real* website and report the phishing attempt!

» **Include personal information in an Internet newsgroup or social media post.** (A *newsgroup* is a public Internet message base, often called a *Usenet group.* Most ISPs offer a selection of newsgroups that you can download.) Newsgroup posts can be viewed by anyone with a newsgroup account (or through sites like Google Groups), so there's no such thing as privacy in a newsgroup. Likewise, social media like Facebook and Twitter are great for communicating with friends and family, but it's simply a bad idea to include personal information in your posts.

» **Buy from an online store that doesn't offer a secure, encrypted connection when you're prompted for your personal information and credit card number.** If you're using the Apple Safari browser, the padlock icon appears next to the site name in the Address box at the top center of the Safari window. When the padlock icon appears in the window and the web address begins with the `https` prefix, the connection is encrypted and secure.

» **Divulge personal information to others over a Messages connection.** I tell you more about Messages in Chapter 16.

» **Use the same password for all your electronic business.** Use different passwords that include both letters and numbers and change them often, and never divulge them to anyone else.

Chapter 14
Browsing the Web with Safari

Navigating the web is easy, but you need a browser to visit your favorite sites. On your Mac, that browser is Safari, of course, and it just keeps getting better with each new version. It doesn't matter whether you're working wirelessly from a hotel room or the comfort of your home: Safari delivers the web the right way. You can

» Search for information, display sites you visited, and navigate to your favorite sites.

» Download files and print documents.

» Mark articles for later perusal.

» Block irritating pop-up windows.

» Customize the program to match your preferences.

In this chapter, I assume that you're using Safari as your browser. Most of what you'll find here, however, is similar to what you'll find in other popular browsers, such as Google Chrome.

Visit a Website

To begin your travels around the Internet, follow these steps:

1. Launch Safari by clicking the Safari compass icon on the Dock. The Safari window opens and displays your home page.

Your *home page* is the initial website you see every time you launch Safari, so most folks change their home page to a favorite location on the web. (Mine, for example, is set to CNN because I'm a newshound.) I show you how to change your home page later in the chapter, in the section "Set Up a Home Page."

TIP

2. Click in the Address and Search text box, shown in **Figure 14-1**; type the address of the website you want to visit; and then press Return. The page appears in the Content window, which occupies most of the Safari window.

Some website addresses still begin with the www. prefix and end with the .com suffix, but often, you'll encounter addresses that begin or end differently. Make sure to enter the web address exactly as it appears in advertisements, email messages, or news reports!

TIP

Navigation toolbar   **Address box**

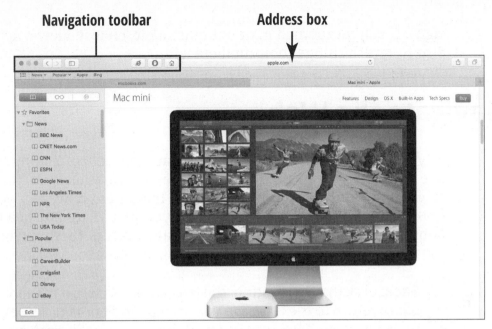

FIGURE 14-1

3. On the resulting web page, click an underlined (or highlighted) link to continue web surfing. Many pictures are also links as well. Whenever your cursor turns into a gloved hand, your cursor is hovering over a link. Often, links are underlined, typically in blue (if you haven't clicked it) or purple (if you have). You can also switch directly to another page by returning to Step 2.

Safari also launches automatically when you

» Click a page link in Apple Mail or another Internet application.

» Click a Safari web page icon on the Dock, on the Desktop, or in a Finder window.

» Click a website within the Contacts application.

TIP

If your eyesight isn't perfect — I'm wearing glasses as I type this — you'll appreciate Safari's Zoom feature, which increases the size of text and graphics displayed by web pages. Choose View⟹Zoom In to zoom in on the contents or press ⌘++ (the plus sign). To zoom back out, choose View⟹Zoom Out or press ⌘+− (the minus sign). If you've zoomed in or out quite a bit, choose View ⇨ Actual Size to return things to normal quickly.

Navigate the Web

A typical web surfing session is a linear experience: You move from one page to the next, absorbing the information you want and discarding the rest. After you visit a few sites, however, you may find that you want to return to a site you just visited or head to the familiar ground of your home page. Safari offers these navigational controls on the toolbar, as shown in **Figure 14-2**:

» **Back:** Click the Back button (the left-facing arrow) on the toolbar to return to the last page you visited. Additional clicks open previous pages in reverse order. The Back button is disabled (ghostly and grayed out) if you haven't visited at least two sites.

» **Forward:** If you clicked the Back button at least once, clicking the Forward button (the right-facing arrow) opens the next page (or pages) where you were, in forward order. The Forward button is disabled (again, ghostly) if you haven't used the Back button.

» **Reload/Stop:** Click the Reload button (a circular arrow) at the right side of the Address and Search box to *refresh*, or reload, the contents of the current page. Although most pages remain static, some pages (like CNN or stock tickers) change their content at regular intervals or after you fill out a form or click a button. By clicking Reload, you can see what's changed on these pages. While a page is loading, the Reload button turns into the Stop button — with a little X mark on it — and you can click it to stop loading the content from the current page.

TIP

You can choose which icons appear on your Safari toolbar. Choose View ⇨ Customize Toolbar, drag the icon you want, and then drop it in the desired spot on the toolbar. (Remember to click and hold while moving the icon to drag it.) To remove an icon from your Safari toolbar, drag the offending icon off the toolbar and release.

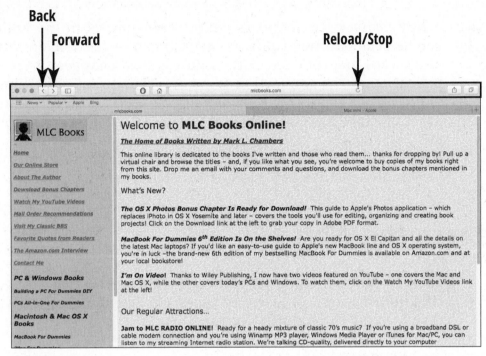

FIGURE 14-2

I discuss four other Safari toolbar icons in more detail later in this chapter. *Note:* Not all of these icons appear on the default toolbar, so you may need to add an icon or two, as I describe in the preceding Tip.

» **Home:** Click this button (look for the little house) to return to your home page.

» **Share:** Click this toolbar button (carries a square-and-arrow icon) to add a bookmark, add the page to your Reading List, email a page to someone, post the page to social-media sites, or create a note or reminder.

» **Print:** Click this button (which bears a printer icon) to print the contents of the Safari window.

» **Address and Search:** As I mention earlier, you can type a web-site address directly in this box, but you can also type text to search Google, Yahoo!, or Bing (all popular search engines) for a subject or site available on the web. (People use these search engines to find everything from used auto parts to former spouses.)

TIP

A tiny padlock icon appears next to the address in the Address and Search box when you're connected to a secure website. You'll also notice that the `http` in the Address field changes to `https` to indicate that the connection is secure. This is A Good Thing! A *secure site* encrypts the information you send and receive, making it much harder for other people to steal credit-card numbers and personal information, for example. *Never* — I mean *never* — enter any valuable personal or financial information on a web page unless you see the secure-connection padlock symbol.

Search the Web

Looking for something in particular on the web? We all need specific information from time to time, and Safari makes it easy to use Google to dig through the entire web:

1. Launch Safari.

2. Click the Address and Search box, and type the text that you want to find on the web. Safari immediately displays a list of possible matches, as shown in **Figure 14-3**.

TIP

You can search for a specific name or phrase by enclosing it within quotes, such as "Louis Armstrong" or "combustion engine." Otherwise, you'd get *hits* (possible sources) on Louis, and Armstrong, and Louis Armstrong. Too many.

List of possible matches

FIGURE 14-3

3. Click any of the entries in the list to open the search-engine page.

4. Click an underlined link on the search-engine page to jump to that web page.

TIP

To repeat a recent search, click the magnifying-glass icon in the Address and Search box and select your search term from the pop-up menu.

Find Content on a Web Page

If you're looking for specific text on the web page currently displayed in Safari, there's no reason to manually scan the entire contents of the page! Instead, use Safari's Find feature to locate every occurrence of that text within the page. Follow these steps:

1. After displaying in the Safari window the web page you want to search, press ⌘+F (or choose Edit ➪ Find ➪ Find). Safari displays the Find bar (which appears directly below the toolbar).

2. Type the word or phrase you're looking for in the Find box; you don't need to press Return. Safari highlights any matches it finds, as shown in **Figure 14-4**.

3. Click the Next button on the Find bar (it carries a right-arrow icon) to advance to each spot within the page in order, all the way to the bottom of the page. To search upward to the top of the page, click the Previous button (which bears a left-arrow icon).

4. When you're finished searching, click the Done button.

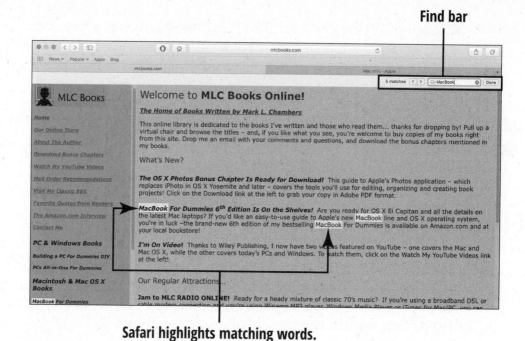

Find bar

Safari highlights matching words.

FIGURE 14-4

Add Pages to the Reading List

Safari includes a Reading List, where you can store pages until you have time to read them. To use the Reading List, follow these steps:

1. While viewing a page, click the Share icon at the right side of the Safari toolbar (the square icon with the arrow) and choose Add to Reading List. Alternatively, choose Bookmarks ⇨ Add to Reading List.

2. When you're ready to read the article, click the Show Sidebar button at the left end of the Safari toolbar and click the Reading List tab (which bears an eyeglasses icon).

3. Choose View ⇨ Show Reading List Sidebar. Safari displays the Reading List pane on the left side of the window, as shown in **Figure 14-5**.

4. To view a page, click its thumbnail in the Reading List.

TIP

Hide the Reading List pane by clicking the toolbar icon again while you continue browsing, or leave the pane open.

Show Reading List icon

Reading List pane

FIGURE 14-5

When you're finished reading the page, remove it from your list. Just hover your pointer over the item and click the Delete button that appears in the top-right corner of the thumbnail (an X symbol). To delete all pages from your list, right-click any Reading List item and choose Clear All from the shortcut menu.

Set Up a Home Page

Tired of using `www.apple.com` as your home page? You can easily choose a different web page that you check often during the day or even open Safari with a blank page. Follow these steps:

1. Display the web page you want as your new home page in Safari. (I recommend selecting a page with few graphics or a fast-loading popular site.)

2. Choose Safari ➪ Preferences or press ⌘+, (comma).

3. Click the General button to display the General pane, as shown in **Figure 14-6**.

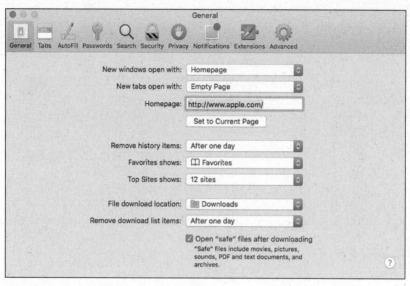

FIGURE 14-6

4. Click the Set to Current Page button.

TIP

To set a blank page (for the fastest window display), click the New Windows Open With pop-up menu and choose Empty Page.

5. Click the Close button to close the Preferences dialog.

Bookmark a Website

You can set up *bookmarks* within Safari that make it easy to jump directly to your favorite pages. (Unlike pages in your Reading List, bookmarks are meant to remain after you visit the page; you can return to bookmarked pages in future browsing sessions.) To book-mark a website, follow these steps:

1. Launch Safari, and navigate to a page.

2. Choose Bookmarks ⇨ Add Bookmark or press the ⌘+D keyboard shortcut. (You can also click the Share button on the toolbar and

choose Add Bookmark from the menu that appears.) Safari displays a sheet where you can enter the name for the bookmark and also select where it appears (on the Bookmarks bar, which appears right below the toolbar, or the Bookmarks menu at the top of the window).

3. Type a name, and choose where to store the bookmark from the drop-down menu.

TIP

The Bookmarks menu includes both its own bookmark entries and a submenu for the Bookmarks bar entries (Bookmarks ➪ Bookmarks Bar), so you can reach both sets of bookmarks from the menu.

4. Click Add.

To find all your bookmarks, choose Bookmarks ➪ Show Bookmarks. (Alternatively, click the Show Sidebar button on the toolbar and click the Bookmark tab.) The Bookmarks pane in the sidebar (see **Figure 14-7**) displays everything in the Bookmarks bar and menu, as well as any bookmark folders you've created.

Show All Bookmarks icon

Bookmarks organized in a folder

Collections pane

FIGURE 14-7

Organize Bookmarks

The more bookmarks you add, the more unwieldy the Bookmarks menu and the Bookmarks pane become. To keep your bookmarks organized, follow these steps to create folders or do a little spring-cleaning:

1. With Safari open, choose Bookmarks ⇨ Add Bookmark Folder.

2. Type a name for the new folder, and press Return.

3. Drag bookmarks into the new folder to help reduce the clutter.

4. To delete a bookmark or a folder from the Collections pane, right-click it and choose Remove from the shortcut menu.

To choose a bookmark from within a folder, display the Bookmarks pane and click the folder in the list at the left; then click the desired bookmark.

View Your Browsing History

To keep track of sites you've visited, you can display the History list. Your browsing history is the tool of choice when you want to quickly return to a site that you recently visited (but haven't bookmarked or added to your Reading List). Follow these steps:

1. With Safari open, click the History menu.

2. To return to a page in the list, choose it from the History menu, as shown in **Figure 14-8**.

3. Hover your cursor over past dates to display the sites you visited on those days, and click to jump to a page.

If you're not keen on keeping a list of where you've been, see the later section "Delete History Files."

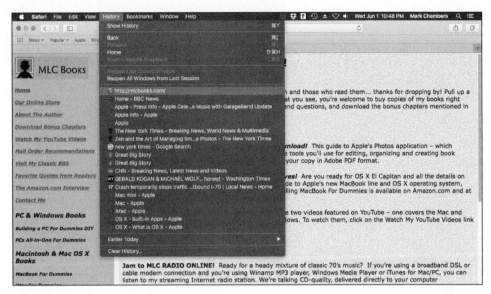

FIGURE 14-8

Use Tabs

Safari also offers *tabbed browsing*, which many folks use to display (and organize) multiple web pages at one time. If you're doing a bit of comparison-shopping for a new piece of hardware at different online stores, tabs are ideal. Follow these steps:

1. With Safari open, hold down the ⌘ key and click a link or bookmark to open a tab for the new page (which appears below the Bookmarks bar).

TIP

You can also choose File ➪ New Tab or press ⌘+T to work the same magic.

2. Click a tab at any time to switch to that page, as shown in **Figure 14-9**. You can remove a tabbed page by hovering your cursor over the tab and clicking the X button next to the tab's title.

TIP

To change settings for tabbed browsing (such as setting Safari to always open new web pages in tabs rather than windows), choose Safari ➪ Preferences to display the Preferences dialog and then click Tabs.

Open tabs

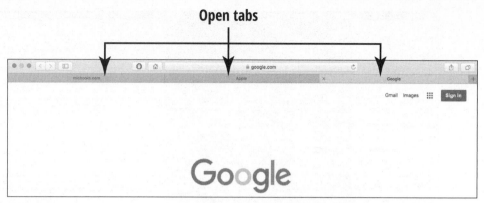

FIGURE 14-9

Download Files

If you visited a site that offers files for downloading, click the Download button or the Download File link, and Safari takes care of the rest. You see the Downloads pop-up list, which keeps you updated on the progress of the transfer. While the file is downloading, feel free to continue browsing or even download additional files; the Downloads list helps you keep track of what's going on and when everything will finish transferring. You can view the Downloads list at any time by clicking the Show Downloads button in the top-right corner of the window (which carries a down-arrow symbol) or by choosing View⇨Show Downloads.

TIP

By default, Safari saves any downloaded files to your OS X Downloads folder on the Dock. To change this setting, choose Safari⇨Preferences and click the General button. Then click the File Download Location pop-up menu and select a new location.

To download a picture that appears on a web page, right-click the picture and choose Save Image As from the shortcut menu that appears. Safari prompts you for the location where you want to store the file. To save the picture directly to your Downloads folder on the Dock, choose Save Image to Downloads from the shortcut menu.

When a file has finished downloading, it remains in the Downloads list, but you can click the Clear button in the list to delete all successfully downloaded entries.

Keep Your Finances Safe Online

Unfortunately, no list of "absolutely safe" online banks or investment companies exists. Online security is a concept you should constantly monitor while exchanging information with websites, especially when that information includes personal data such as your Social Security number and credit-card information.

Keep these guidelines in mind while using online commerce sites to greatly reduce the risk of identity theft (or worse):

» **Never use an online bank or investment house that doesn't offer a secure, encrypted connection when you enter your personal information and credit card number.** If you're using Apple's Safari browser, the padlock icon appears next to the site name in the Address and Search box. When the padlock icon appears, the connection is encrypted and secure (and the address starts with the prefix https rather than http). If the connection isn't secure, *go elsewhere.*

» **Avoid using Safari's AutoFill feature.** If you fill out many forms online — when you're shopping at websites, for example, or trading online — you can add the AutoFill button (which looks like a little text box and a pen) to your toolbar. AutoFill can complete these online forms for you. To be honest, however, I'm not a big fan of releasing *any* of my personal information to *any* website, so I never use AutoFill. You can specify which information is used for AutoFill (or disable it entirely) by launching Safari and choosing Safari ➪ Preferences. Clicking the AutoFill toolbar button in the Preferences dialog displays the settings; to disable AutoFill, just clear each check box.

TIP

If you decide to use this feature, make sure that the connection is secure (again, look for the padlock icon in the Address and Search box) and read the site's Privacy Agreement page first to see how your identity data will be treated.

>> **Look for a security symbol.** Several well-respected online security companies act as watchdogs for online banking and investing institutions. When you see the symbol of one of these companies, it's a good indicator that the bank or broker is interested in maintaining your privacy and protecting your identity. Some of the best-known security companies on the web include TraceSecurity (`www.tracesecurity.com`), Verisign (`www.verisign.com`), and WebSense (`www.forcepoint.com`). Luckily, you don't have to implement all the software and assorted protection protocols that run behind the scenes when you connect to your bank!

Delete History Files

Your History file leaves a clear set of footprints indicating where you've been on the web. Maybe you don't want everyone to know you've been spending all your free time checking out *World of Warcraft* online. If so, you can clear your browser history. To do so, choose History ⇨ Clear History.

Safari also allows you to specify a length of time to retain entries in your History file. Choose Safari ⇨ Preferences, click the General tab, and then click the Remove History Items pop-up menu to specify a length of time. Items can be rolled off daily, weekly, biweekly, monthly, or yearly. Click Manually to keep your History file until you decide to clear it.

Delete Cookie Files

A *cookie* (a ridiculous term) is a small file that a website automatically saves on your hard drive, containing information that the site will use on your future visits. Unfortunately, for these purposes, cookies aren't yummy treats made from flour, sugar, butter, and eggs. A site might save a cookie to preserve your site preferences for the next visit or — in the case of a site such as Amazon.com — to identify you automatically and help customize the offerings you see.

In and of themselves, cookies aren't bad things. Unlike viruses, cookie files don't replicate themselves or wreak havoc on your system, and only the original site can read the cookie it creates. Many folks, however, don't appreciate acting as gracious hosts for a slew of little snippets of personal information.

You can choose to accept all cookies — the default setting — or opt to disable cookies. You can also set Safari to accept cookies only from the sites you choose to visit. To change your *cookie acceptance plan* (or CAP, if you absolutely crave acronyms), click the Safari icon on the Dock and follow these steps:

1. Choose Safari ➪ Preferences.

2. Click the Privacy button. Safari displays the Privacy preference settings, as shown in **Figure 14-10**.

Most Mac users should select this cookie option.

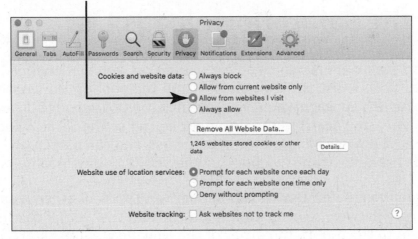

FIGURE 14-10

3. Choose how to block cookies (select one radio button):

- *Allow from Websites I Visit:* I use this option, which allows sites such as Amazon.com to work correctly without allowing a barrage of illicit cookies.

- *Allow from Current Website Only:* Block cookies from everywhere but those that operate on the current site.

- *Always Block:* Block all cookies.

- *Always Allow:* Accept all cookies, which essentially allows any site to save cookies on your Mac.

4. To view the cookies now on your system, click the Details button. To remove all cookies and data, click the Remove All Website Data button.

TIP

If you block all cookies, you may have to take care of some tasks manually, such as providing a password on the site that used to be read automatically from the cookie.

5. Click the Close button to save your changes.

Delete the Safari Downloads List

Safari makes it easy to clear the list of files you've downloaded over time. The file list is maintained within the pop-up Downloads window, which appears whenever you click the Downloads button (bears a down-arrow icon) in the top-right corner of the Safari window. (If you have downloads remaining in the list, you can display the Downloads list at any time by choosing View ⇨ Show Downloads.)

To keep your Safari Downloads list tidy (and prevent other people from seeing what you've been pulling down from the web), click the Clear button in the top-right corner of the Downloads list. Safari removes any entries for downloaded items you've successfully received.

Print a Web Page

Many web pages have a button you can click to print the page. If you want to print a page and it doesn't have a Print button or link, follow these steps:

1. Click the Print button on the toolbar, choose File ⇨ Print, or press ⌘+P.

2. Click the Printer pop-up menu and choose the printer you want to use, as shown in **Figure 14-11**.

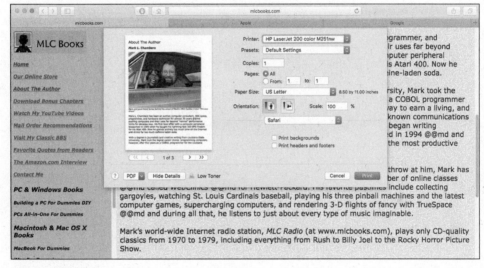

FIGURE 14-11

3. When you're ready to print the pages, click Print.

TIP

If you choose to print pages from a website, I recommend that you preview the pages first. Unfortunately, the complex design of many websites may result in the wrong text being printed, or pages produced that are impossible to read. I usually create a PDF file of the pages instead by clicking the PDF drop-down menu on the Print dialog and choosing Save as PDF (that way, you won't waste paper if the results aren't up to snuff).

Chapter 15
Using Mail

O S X includes quite a capable and reliable email client — Apple Mail (affectionately called Mail by everyone except Bill Gates). Mail provides all you need to

» Send and receive email messages.

» Screen junk mail from your inbox.

» Receive and send attachments.

» Update your Contacts database with new email contacts.

» Organize your mail by using folders.

Naturally, your Mac needs to be connected to the Internet before email starts flying into your inbox. If you haven't set up your Internet connection yet, visit Chapter 13 for all the details.

Set Up an Internet Email Account

Most Mac owners choose one of three sources for an Internet email account:

> » **An existing Internet service provider (ISP):** If you're signed up with an ISP (including local cable companies and DSL providers), that company almost certainly will provide you at least one email address as part of your service. Contact your ISP for your email account information. Popular ISPs include Mediacom, AOL, and Charter.

> » **Apple's iCloud online service:** iCloud members receive free email service from Apple. Your iCloud email address should be yourname@me.com, where yourname is the username you chose when you subscribed. (I go into more detail on iCloud, Apple's free Internet service for storing and syncing all kinds of data, in Chapter 13.)

> » **A web-based email provider:** Many sites on the web offer free email services, such as Google Gmail, Yahoo! Mail, and Microsoft Outlook.com. You can sign up for these email accounts online. (I use and recommend Google Gmail, which you can access at www.google.com. Just click the Gmail link at the top of the page to start the sign-up process. If you're already using an iPhone or iPad with a Gmail account, you can use the Gmail address you've already set up.)

Apple Mail can accommodate most email services, no matter where they're hosted.

If you already have an existing email account that you use with Windows Mail, Microsoft Outlook, or Outlook Express on your PC, you can use that account easily under Apple Mail.

TIP

Note that iCloud email accounts are set up automatically for you within Apple Mail, so you typically don't have to follow the process outlined in the next section for your iCloud account.

Set Up an Apple Mail Account

After you set up an email account with your ISP or another provider, you need to add that account so that Apple Mail can access it.

Follow these steps to add an account to Apple Mail:

1. Launch Mail from the Dock by clicking the icon that looks like a postage stamp.

2. If the Add Account Assistant doesn't automatically appear, as shown in **Figure 15-1**, choose Mail ➪ Add Account to display it.

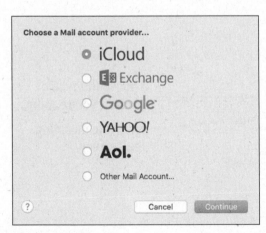

FIGURE 15-1

TIP

3. Click the email service provider for this account or, if your provider doesn't appear in the list, click Other Mail Account.

4. Click Continue.

Here's a neat trick: If Mail can immediately recognize an email service, such as Google Mail, it attempts to set up that account for you automatically. (Because each service requires different information, the Add Account Assistant provides onscreen instructions.) If the setup and testing are successful, you can skip the rest of these steps!

5. If you clicked Other Mail Account in Step 4, type your full name, and then the email address and the password assigned to you by your ISP. (Mail uses the email address and password to log in to your ISP and retrieve your messages.)

6. Click Sign In.

Again, Mail attempts to automatically set up your account. If the setup and testing are successful, you're done!

If Mail is unable to set up your account automatically, you see the sheet displayed in **Figure 15-2**.

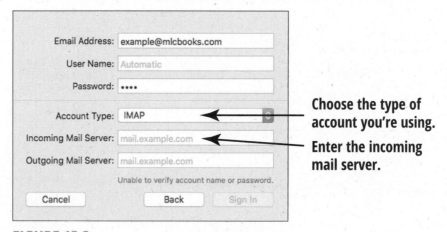

Choose the type of account you're using.

Enter the incoming mail server.

FIGURE 15-2

7. Click the Account Type box, and choose the type of account you're using (typically POP for most free services, including Gmail and Microsoft's Outlook.com).

8. Click the Incoming Mail Server text box, and type your incoming server address.

9. Click the Outgoing Mail Server text box, and type the outgoing server address.

Your email provider should provide this information. If you're unclear what goes where, I recommend placing a telephone call to the ISP's technical support number.

10. Click Sign In.

Get to Know Apple Mail

Figure 15-3 illustrates the Mail window. Besides the familiar toolbar, which naturally carries buttons specific to Mail, you find these elements:

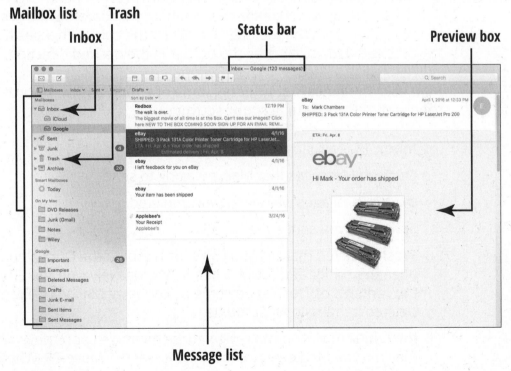

FIGURE 15-3

» **Status bar:** This heading bar at the top of the Mail window displays information about the current folder — typically, how many messages it contains, but other data can be included.

» **Message list:** This box contains all the messages for the chosen folder.

TIP

You can sort the messages in the message list by choosing them from the View menu or by clicking the Sort By pop-up menu that appears at the top of the list. (By default, messages are sorted by date.)

» **Mailboxes:** The sidebar on the left side of the main Mail window contains the Mailboxes list. (It's helpful to think of a mailbox within Mail as a group of folders tied to one account.) Click any of the folders to switch the display in the message list. You can show or hide the mailbox list by choosing View ⇨ Show/Hide Mailbox List, or you can press the ⌘+Shift+M keyboard shortcut.

» **Preview pane:** This resizable pane displays the contents of the selected message, including both text and any graphics or attachments that Mail recognizes. To make the preview pane larger or smaller, move your cursor over the border separating the preview pane from the message list. When the cursor changes to a double-sided arrow, drag the border in the desired direction.

Mail uses the following folders (some of which appear only at certain times, or with certain account settings):

» **Inbox:** Mail already received.

» **Outbox:** Messages that Mail is waiting to send.

» **Drafts:** Messages waiting to be completed.

» **Sent:** Mail you sent already.

» **Trash:** Deleted mail. As you can with Trash on the Dock, you can open this folder and retrieve items. Alternatively, you can empty the contents of Trash at any time by choosing Mailbox ⇨ Erase Deleted Items ⇨ In All Accounts.

» **Junk:** Junk mail. You can review these messages or retrieve any that you want to keep by choosing Message ⇨ Move To. When you're sure that nothing of value is left, you can send the remaining messages straight to the Trash. (Junk-mail filtering must be enabled before you see this option; more on this later in this chapter.)

Manage Email Accounts

Choose Mail⇨Preferences and click the Accounts tab to display the Accounts pane, shown in **Figure 15-4**. There, you can add a Mail account, edit an existing account, or remove an account. Although many folks still have only one email account, you can use a passel of them. You might use one account for your personal email and one account for your business correspondence, for example. To switch accounts, choose the account you want to use from this list to make it the active account.

Your email accounts   **Change your name.**

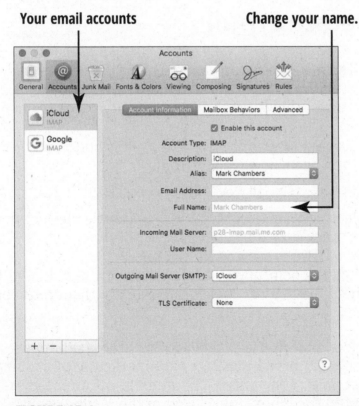

FIGURE 15-4

You can also edit any field on the Account Information tab. If you decide to change your email From name, for example, click the Full Name text box, press the Delete key to erase the existing name, and then type a new name.

Sometimes, you can't reach one of your accounts. Maybe you're vacationing with your MacBook and can't access your ISP's mail server directly. To avoid all the error messages and futile attempts to connect to an email provider you can't reach, Apple Mail lets you enable and disable specific accounts without enduring the hassle of deleting an account and then adding it again.

To disable or enable an account, choose Mail ⇨ Preferences to open the Preferences dialog, and click the Accounts tab. Select an account and then select (or deselect) the Enable This Account check box as necessary.

Read and Delete Email

The heart and soul of Mail — at least the heart, anyway — is receiving and reading stuff from your friends and family. After your account is set up, use any of these methods to manually check for new mail:

» Click the Get New Messages from All Accounts button on the toolbar (which bears an envelope icon).

» Choose Mailbox ⇨ Get All New Mail or press ⌘+Shift+N.

» Choose Mailbox ⇨ Get New Mail and then choose the specific account to check from the submenu.

TIP

The last method is a helpful way to check for new mail in another account without having to make it active in the Preferences window.

If you have new mail in the active account, the mail appears in the Message list. New, unread messages are marked with a snazzy blue dot on the left side of the entry. The number of unread messages is displayed next to the inbox-folder icon in the Mailboxes list.

TIP

Mail also displays on its Dock icon the number of unread messages you received. If you hid the Mail window or sent it to the Dock, you can perform a quick visual check for new mail by glancing at the Dock.

To read any message in the message list, you can click to select an entry (which displays the contents of the message in the preview box) or double-click the entry to open the message in a separate window.

To skim your mail, click the first message that you want to view in the list and then press the down-arrow key when you're ready to move to the next message. Mail displays the content of each message in the preview box. To display the previous message in the list, press the up-arrow key.

TIP

If your vision isn't what it once was, why not let Mail *read* you your mail? Simply select one message or a group of messages and then choose Edit ⇨ Speech ⇨ Start Speaking. *Wowsers!*

To delete a message from the message list, click an entry to select it and then click the Delete button on the toolbar (or press the Del key on the keyboard). You can also right-click any message entry in the list and choose Delete from the menu that appears. To delete a message from within a message window, click the Delete button on the toolbar.

Reply to a Message

Replying to a message you receive is easy. Follow these steps:

1. Click to select a message entry in the message list and then click the Reply button on the Mail toolbar (which bears a single arrow curving to the left).

TIP

To respond to a message that you opened in a message window, click the Reply button on the toolbar for the message window.

If a message was addressed not just to you, but also to several other people, you can send your reply to all recipients. Just click the Reply

All button on the Mail window toolbar (it bears *two* arrows curving to the left). This technique is a useful way to quickly facilitate a festive gathering, if you get my drift.

Mail opens the Reply window, as shown in **Figure 15-5**. Note that the address has been added automatically and that the default Subject is Re: *<the original subject>*. Mail automatically adds a separator line in the message body field that reads On *<day><date>at<time>*, *<addressee>* wrote:, followed by the text of the original message. The original text is indented and prefaced by a vertical line to set it apart.

(Optional) Click in the Subject line and change the default Subject line; otherwise, the flashing cursor is already sitting on the first line of the text box.

Send your message.   **Attach a file.**

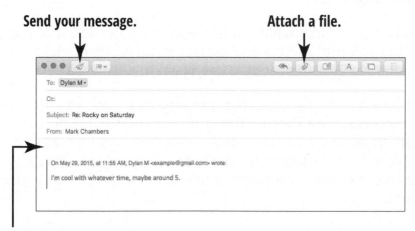

Begin typing your reply.

FIGURE 15-5

2. Start typing your reply in the text box.

3. (Optional) When you complete your reply, you can select text in the message body and apply different fonts or formats.

   See "Format Email Messages," later in this chapter, for more information.

4. (Optional) To add an attachment, click the Attach button on the Reply window toolbar (which bears a paper-clip icon).

See the upcoming sections "Send an Attachment" and "Save an Attachment That You Receive" for the full lowdown on attachments.

5. When you're ready to send your reply, you have two options:

- *Click the Send button (bearing the nifty paper airplane icon) to send the message immediately.*

- *Choose File ⇨ Save (or press ⌘+S) to store it in your Drafts folder for later editing.*

Saving the message to your Drafts folder isn't the same as sending it. You can save the message for a while so that you can come back and finish it later. To send a message held in your Drafts folder, click the Drafts folder in the Mailboxes list and then double-click the message you want to send. Mail displays the message window — you can make edits at this point, if you like — and then click the Send button on the message window toolbar.

When you reply to a message, you can also *forward* your reply to another person (rather than the original sender). The new addressee receives a message containing both the text of the original message you received and your reply. To forward a message, click the Forward button (which bears a right-facing arrow) rather than Reply or Reply All on the Mail toolbar.

TIP

Create and Send Email

To compose and send a new message to someone else, follow these steps:

1. Click the New Message button on the Mail toolbar (which bears a pencil-and-paper icon).

You can also choose File ⇨ New Message or avail yourself of the handy ⌘+N keyboard shortcut.

Mail opens the New Message window, as shown in **Figure 15-6**.

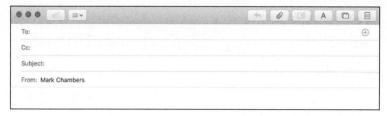

FIGURE 15-6

2. Enter the recipient's (To) address by taking one of these actions:

   - Type it directly in the To field.

   - Paste it after copying it to the Clipboard, which I discuss in Chapter 8.

   - Drag an email address from your Contacts application. (Read all about how to add contacts by using Mail, later in this chapter.)

   - Click the Add button (bearing a plus sign) on the right side of the window. Mail shows you the Contacts window, as shown in **Figure 15-7**. The Contacts window displays the contacts you have in your Contacts application that include an email address. Click to select the address you want to use. To pick multiple recipients, open the Contacts window again.

3. (Optional) To send "carbon" copies of the message to additional recipients, click the Cc field.

   Again, you can type the addresses directly, use the contents of the Clipboard, or display the Contacts window.

4. Click the Subject field, enter the subject of the message, and then press Tab twice.

   The text cursor now rests in the first line of the message text box, and you're ready to type your message, my friend!

5. Type your message in the message box.

6. (Optional) Click the Show Stationery button at the far right end of the message window toolbar to display the Stationery pane above the message text box, and choose one of the many email message backgrounds that Apple supplies.

Add button

FIGURE 15-7

Stationery isn't required, but it truly packs a visual wallop! Click a thumbnail on the strip to add it to your message; to display a different stationery category, such as a Greeting or Invitation, click the category buttons on the left side of the Stationery pane.

TIP

Not all email applications on other computers correctly display a message with a stationery background, so if a recipient can't open or read the message, avoid sending stationery to that person in the future. Also, it's important to note that adding a stationery background significantly increases the message size (and, therefore, the transfer time to send and receive it, especially over a dial-up modem connection).

7. (Optional) When you finish typing your message, you can select text in the message body and apply different fonts or formats.

I cover formatting in "Format Email Messages," later in this chapter.

8. (Optional) To add an attachment, click the Attach button on the message window toolbar.

Attachments are described in the following section.

9. When you're ready to send, click the Send button to send the message immediately, or press ⌘+S to store the message in your Drafts folder.

Send an Attachment

Attachments are a fun way to transfer files by email. However, you must remember these three vital caveats:

TIP

» **Attachments can contain viruses.** Even a message attachment that was sent by your best friend can contain a virus — either because your friend unwittingly passed one along or because the virus took control of your friend's email application and replicated itself automatically. (Ugh.)

Never — I mean *never* — send or receive attachments unless you have an up-to-date antivirus scanning application running. I discuss antivirus applications in Chapter 13.

» **Corpulent attachments don't make it.** Most ISP mail servers have a 10–20MB limit for the total size of a message, and the attachment counts toward that final message size. Therefore, I recommend sending a file as an attachment only if it's smaller than 10MB. If the recipient's email server sends you an automated message saying that the message was refused because it was too big, this is the problem. To display a file's size before you send it, right-click the file's icon and choose Get Info from the shortcut menu. (A typical JPEG is about 1MB, so it's a good idea to send no more than five or six photos at once.)

» **Not all email applications accept attachments.** Not all email programs support attachments in the same way, and other email programs are simply set for pure text messages. If the message recipient receives the message text but not the attachment, these are the likely reasons.

With that said, it's back to attachments as a beneficial feature.

While replying to a message (or creating a new message), you can add an attachment by clicking the Attach button on the toolbar; it's the one with the paper clip.

Mail displays a File Open sheet. Navigate to a file, select it, and click the Choose File button to add the file to the message.

If the recipient is running Windows, click the Options button and make sure that the Send Windows–Friendly Attachments check box is selected. This results in a slightly larger email message but helps ensure that PC email programs, such as Outlook and Windows Mail, can correctly open your attachments.

Save an Attachment That You Receive

Sometimes, you don't want to save (download) attachments that people send to you. If Cousin Fred sends you a funny cartoon that you chuckle at but don't really need to save, you can safely delete it. But what if someone sends you an attachment, such as a picture of your grandkids, that you truly want to hang on to? Follow these steps to save an attachment that you receive in a message:

1. Click the message with an attachment in your message list.

   If you're having trouble determining which messages have attachments, choose View ⇨ Message Attributes and then choose the Attachments option from the submenu that appears to toggle it on. Now every message with an attachment appears with a tiny paper-clip icon displayed to the left of the entry.

   If Mail recognizes the attachment format, it displays or plays the attachment in the body of the message; if not, the attachment is displayed as a file icon.

2. To open an attachment that's displayed as a file icon, right-click the icon and choose Open Attachment from the shortcut menu.

3. To save an attachment, right-click the attachment (however it appears in the message) and choose Save Attachment from the shortcut menu.

4. In the Save dialog that appears, navigate to the location where you want to save the file. If necessary, you can click in the text box and change the filename to something you'll recognize. Click Save to store the attachment in the location you specified.

Format Email Messages

Why settle for a boring, plain-text message when you can add special fonts and colors? Mail makes it easy to format your messages, much as you format text in a Pages document. As I mentioned earlier, a handful of email applications accept only simple text in a message, but most Mac and Windows email applications can display basic formatting with ease.

To change text formatting, select the text and choose Format ⇨ Show Fonts. From the window that appears, you can choose the font family, type size, and formatting (such as italic or bold) for the selected text. Click the Close button on the Fonts window to continue.

To apply color to selected text, choose Format ⇨ Show Colors and then click anywhere in the color wheel that appears to select that color. You can also vary the hue by moving the slider bar at the bottom of the Colors window. After you find the color that expresses your inner passion, click the Close button in the Colors window to continue.

Add Contacts

El Capitan comes equipped with a separate Contacts application, which you can run from the Dock or Launchpad. The Contacts works just like the paper variety, allowing you to save all sorts of contact data for each entry. If you receive a message from your niece Harriet, and she isn't in your Contacts database yet, you can easily add her to your contacts from within Apple Mail (rather than manually running Contacts and creating a new entry by hand).

With the message selected in the message list, choose Message➪Add Sender to Contacts. Mail automatically creates a new contact, and the person's name and email address are added automatically to your Contacts database. Could it be any easier?

Customize Apple Mail

Like all other Apple software, Mail is easy to customize to your liking from the Preferences window (shown in **Figure 15-8**).

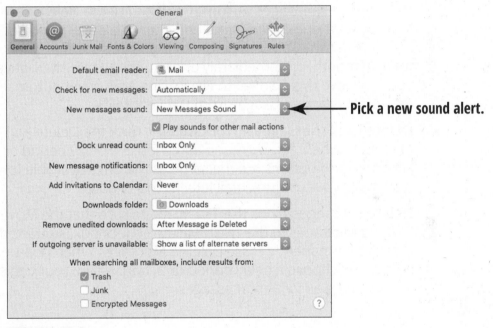

Pick a new sound alert.

FIGURE 15-8

To choose a sound that plays whenever you receive new mail, choose Mail➪Preferences and click the General tab. Click the New Messages Sound pop-up menu and choose one of the sounds that Apple provides. Choose None from the pop-up menu to disable the new mail sound altogether.

To disable automatic mail checking, display the General pane in the Preferences window, click the Check for New Messages pop-up menu and choose Manually; you can click the Get Mail toolbar button to manually check your mail anytime you like. (If you're using a dial-up analog modem connection, you may not fancy Mail's taking control of the telephone line every five minutes.)

If you like, Mail can be set to automatically delete sent mail (and permanently erase messages that you relegate to the Trash). To configure these settings, click the Accounts tab in the Preferences window toolbar, click to select an account, and click the Mailboxes Behaviors button. Then choose what you like in the Sent, Junk and Trash sections of the Preferences window:

» **Delete sent messages automatically:** Click the Delete Sent Messages When pop-up menu and choose a delay period or action. You can choose to delete mail you've sent after a day, a week, a month, or immediately after quitting Mail. Alternatively, you can leave this field set to Never, and Mail never automatically deletes any messages from the Sent folder.

» **Delete junk messages automatically:** Click the Delete Junk Messages When pop-up menu and choose a delay period or action. (These options are the same as the ones available for sent mail.) I discuss junk mail later in this chapter.

» **Delete messages from the Trash:** Make sure that the Move Deleted Messages to the Trash Mailbox check box is selected, click the Permanently Erase Deleted Messages When pop-up menu, and choose a delay period or action. Again, your choices are the same as for sent messages.

Add a Signature to All Outgoing Messages

To add a block of text or a graphical image to the bottom of your messages as your personal signature, follow these steps:

1. Choose Mail ⇨ Preferences and click the Signatures tab on the toolbar.

2. From the Signatures pane that appears, click the Add Signature button (which carries a plus sign) to display the new signature entry you see in **Figure 15-9**.

Type a name for your signature.

Type the text for your signature.

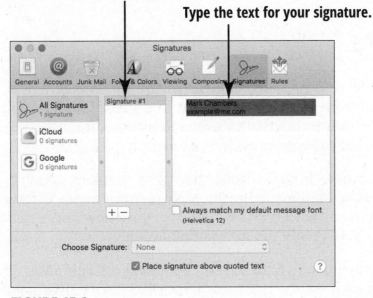

FIGURE 15-9

3. Click the signature name to open an edit box, type an identifying name, and press Return to save the new name.

4. Click inside the text entry box to the right to move the cursor.

5. Type the signature itself in the text entry box, or copy the signature to the Clipboard and paste it into the text entry box.

   TIP

   Because downloading a complex, high-resolution image in a signature takes longer — and because some folks still use plain-text email — I recommend that you avoid the temptation to include graphics in your signature.

6. If you have multiple signatures, click the Choose Signature pop-up menu to choose which one you want to use or to use them all randomly or in sequence.

If you want your signature to appear above the quoted text in a reply, click to select the Place Signature above Quoted Text check box. (In email jargon, *quoted* text refers to the original message text that's inserted into your reply. Mail adds the quoted text so that your recipient can keep track of the continuing discussion!)

Use Folders

You can add new personal folders to the Mailboxes list to further organize your messages. You can put in a special folder all messages from your quilting club that talk about patterns, for example, making it easy to refer to those messages as a group.

To create a new folder within the same mailbox account, choose Mailbox ⇨ New Mailbox from the Mail menu. Choose On My Mac as your location and then type the name for your new folder in the Name box. Click OK to create the new personal folder.

This folder appears in Mail only on your desktop computer. If you check your mail via the Internet or your iOS device (iPhone, iPad, or iPod touch), you won't see this folder.

Messages can be dragged from the message list and dropped into a folder in the Mailboxes list to transfer them. Alternatively, you can move them from the Message list by selecting the messages you want to move, choosing Message ⇨ Move To, and then clicking to select a destination folder.

Handle Junk Mail

Unfortunately, everyone receives junk email (or *spam*) these days, and because chucking the First Amendment is *not* an option, I guess we'll always have it. (Come to think of it, my paper mailbox is just as full of the stuff.)

Fortunately, Apple Mail has a net that you can cast to collect junk mail before you have to read it, as well as a separate Junk folder in your Mailboxes list. (You can view the unscrupulous contents by clicking the Junk folder icon.) The two methods of handling junk mail are

» **Manually:** You can mark any message in the message list as junk mail. Select the unwanted message in the message list and then click the Junk button on the Mail window toolbar, which marks the message as junk. (The Junk button bears a Julius Caesar-style "thumbs-down" icon.) However, the junk message is not automatically moved to the Junk folder when it's marked manually. (If you like, you can drag it there for safekeeping, or it can simply stay in your inbox.) If a message is mistakenly marked as junk, but you want to keep it, click the message to display it in the preview box and then click the Not Junk button at the top of the preview box (or click the Not Junk button on the Mail toolbar, which now sports a thumbs-up icon).

» **Automatically:** Apple Mail has a sophisticated Junk Mail filter that you can train to better recognize junk. (Keep reading to discover how.) After you train Mail to recognize spam with a high degree of accuracy, turn it to full Automatic mode, and it moves all those worthless messages to your Junk folder.

TIP

Note that marking a message in the Junk folder as Not Junk doesn't move it back to the inbox where it was originally received! If you want to restore the inoffensive message to its original inbox (or move it to another folder), drag the message over to the destination in the Mailboxes list.

You customize and train the Junk Mail filter from the Preferences window (available from your trusty Mail menu); click Junk Mail to show the settings. I recommend that you first try the option labeled When Junk Mail Arrives, Mark as Junk Mail but Leave It in My Inbox. This option lets Junk Mail takes its best shot at determining what's junk. When you receive more mail and mark more messages as junk (or mark them as *not* junk), you're teaching the Junk Mail feature how to winnow the wheat from the chaff! Remember that with this setting junk messages aren't moved anywhere; they're just marked with a particularly fitting, grungy brown color, and they stay in your inbox.

When you're satisfied that the Junk Mail filter is catching just about everything it can, display Mail preferences again, and choose the Move It to the Junk Mailbox option. Mail creates a Junk folder and prompts you for permission to move all junk messages to this folder. After you review everything in the Junk folder, you can delete the messages it contains and send them to the Trash folder.

TIP

To save a message from junkdom, click the Not Junk button at the top of the preview pane and then drag the message from the Junk folder message list to a folder in the Mailboxes list.

If you don't receive a lot of spam — or if you want to be *absolutely* sure that nothing is labeled as junk until you review it — click to deselect the Enable Junk Mail Filtering check box. (And good luck.)

TIP

By default, Mail exempts certain messages from Junk Mail status based on three criteria: The sender is in your El Capitan Contacts database, you sent the sender a message in the past, or the message is addressed to you with your full name. To tighten your Junk Mail filtering to the max, you may want to disable these check boxes as well.

To reset the Junk Mail filter and erase any training you gave it, visit the Junk Mail settings in Preferences again and click Reset. Then click the Yes button to confirm your choice.

Chapter 16

Connecting with People Online

Throughout human history, our drive has been to communicate — from the earliest cave paintings to written language and then to the telegraph, the telephone, and the mobile phone (including newer phones that connect to the Internet, let you check email, take photos, play music, and more). I'm here to tell you that your Mac is the ultimate communications device, no matter whom you need to converse with or what the topic may be!

In this chapter, you find out how to

» Chat with someone by typing messages.

» Add to and manage your collection of online friends (otherwise called a Buddy List).

» Start audio and video conversations across the Internet *(chat)*.

» Access online journals *(blogs)* and web discussion groups *(forums)*.

» Start using web meeting sites (social networks) such as Facebook and Twitter.

Check Your Equipment

Forget that silly cellphone and your complicated calling plan! By using your Mac, you can easily chat with your friends and family whether they're across the street or halfway across the world. Here's what you need to get started:

» **Your Mac:** It comes with Messages software preinstalled, allowing you to send and receive instant messages (IM) with other computer users.

» **An Internet connection:** See Chapter 13. For audio or video chat, make sure that you have a broadband connection.

» **A microphone for audio chat and a video camera for video chat:** If you have an iMac computer or a MacBook laptop (the most popular models), you have a built-in microphone for audio chat and a built-in FaceTime video camera for video chat. You're all set. (Some Apple monitors also have cameras and microphones built in.) If you have a MacPro or Mac mini, you need to buy these two devices separately and plug them into the correct port on your Mac; you find all the facts on ports in Chapter 2.

TIP

When you use video chat (in FaceTime or through Messages), you *see* the other person in glorious, full-color video! This fulfills the decades-old promise of the video telephone quite well, thank you. Audio chat is similar to talking on the phone but without the expense of a calling plan. If you haven't used FaceTime yet, it's a full-tilt video chat system, although both sides of the conversation have to be using Apple devices that support FaceTime. (That includes Macs, iPhones, iPads, and iPod touch units.)

Set Up Messages

So why use Messages? When family and friends want to communicate with you by using their computers, they could certainly send email — but that's certainly not immediate, and you'd miss out on hearing or seeing them. Messages allows you to plug into the popular world of Internet instant messaging, which many Mac owners used before through various sources: AOL, Google, Jabber, Yahoo!, Bonjour (between multiple Macs on the same local network) or iMessages (between Apple computers and devices).

Sending a text message to another person is practically instantaneous — hence the name — and many of these services allow you to engage in audio chats (sound only) or video chats (sound and real-time video).

When you first run Messages, you have a little setup work to do. The following steps walk you through the process:

1. Click the Messages icon on the Dock, and you're prompted to create a Messages account. If you decided to not open an iCloud account during the El Capitan setup process, you can still get a free Messages account through Apple. (iCloud is the free online service offered by Apple, which I cover in Chapter 2.)

2. Click the Create Apple ID button, and enter the required information on the Apple web page that appears.

3. In the Account Setup sheet that appears, shown in **Figure 16-1**, follow these steps (depending on which of the following options best fits your situation):

- *You want to use the Apple ID/iCloud account that you set up when you first installed OS X (referred to here as me.com).* In this case, your Apple ID/iCloud account name and password are entered automatically for you, and you're good to go. You can click Cancel on the Account Setup sheet.

Select your account type.

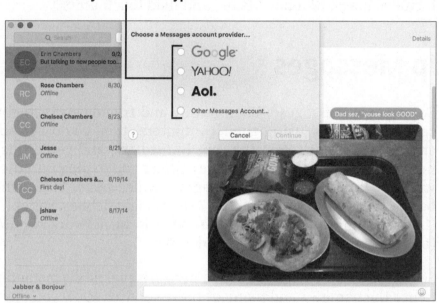

FIGURE 16-1

- *You want to use an existing chat account for AOL, Google, Yahoo!, or Jabber instead:* Click the corresponding Account Type radio button to choose the correct service and click Continue; then enter the account information required for that service.

When you've created an instant messaging account, Messages displays the Messages Buddies window, as shown in **Figure 16-2**. Although this figure shows my list already populated with (my) buddies, a new account will be empty.

TIP

After you configure Messages, you can always run it by clicking its icon on the Dock. From within Launchpad, click the Messages application icon.

A list of your buddies

FIGURE 16-2

Add Friends to Your Messages Buddy List

In Messages, a *buddy* is anyone whom you want to chat with, whether the topic is work or your personal life. Messages keeps track of your buddies in its Buddy List.

TIP

Because Messages is tied closely to the Contacts application, if you have any potential buddies lurking in your Contacts database who have IM accounts, I recommend updating those contacts with their IM account information. (You can simply ask the person you want to add for this information.) It's much easier to allow Messages to pull the account information in automatically while creating a buddy than typing the account names manually!

To add a new buddy, follow these steps:

1. Open Messages by clicking its icon on the Dock.

2. Choose Buddies ➪ Add Buddy to display the Add Buddy sheet, as shown in **Figure 16-3**.

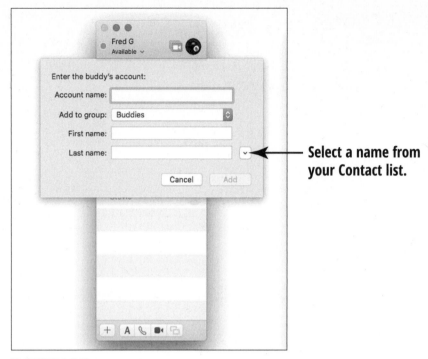

Select a name from your Contact list.

FIGURE 16-3

3. To create a buddy entry from a contact who has an IM username, click the down-arrow button next to the Last Name box to display the contacts list from your Contacts application, and click the entry to select it.

4. To add a person who isn't already in your Contacts database, type the person's IM account name; then click the First Name and Last Name text boxes and type the person's first and last names.

5. Click the Add button to save the buddy information.

TIP

Even when you add a new buddy and that name appears in the Buddy List, don't be concerned if the name literally fades out after a few seconds. The fading just indicates that the person is offline and unavailable. You can also tell when a person is available if her name appears next to a green bullet in the Buddy List. These indicators show a person's status, and your buddies can see your status too. Find out more about status in the next section.

Set Your Status in Messages

Your Messages status lets your Messages buddies know whether you're available to chat. The status options fall into one of two categories:

» **Online:** When you're *online,* folks can invite you to chat and communicate with you.

» **Offline:** When you're *offline,* you're disconnected. Messages isn't active, you can't be paged, and you can't chat.

TIP

Even when you're offline, you can click a buddy name directly, which automatically switches Messages to online mode and opens the paging window for that buddy. (Naturally, you have to have the proper network or Internet connection first.)

Now that you know what's going on behind the scenes, here's the scoop on the live options you can choose among:

» **Available:** You're at your Mac and willing to chat. In addition to plain old Available, Apple provides you some specific choices, such as Surfing the Web.

» **Away:** You can use Away mode whenever Messages is running and you're still online but not available. If I'm away from my Mac for a few minutes, I leave Messages running but switch my status to Away. My buddies see a message saying that I'm away so that they don't bother trying to contact me. Apple also offers a few specific options for Away, too, such as In a Meeting.

» **A custom status:** You, too, can create a custom mode — such as Bored Stiff! or Listening to My Significant Other — and use it rather than the somewhat mundane choice of Available or Away. You find out how to create a custom status later in this section.

To choose an existing mode, follow these steps:

1. Click the Mode button in the Messages Buddies window. (It's below your name at the top of the window, and it should display either your current status or Offline). Messages displays a pop-up menu with your mode choices. Modes with a green bullet are Available modes, and red bullet modes are Away modes. **Figure 16-4** illustrates my custom status choices.

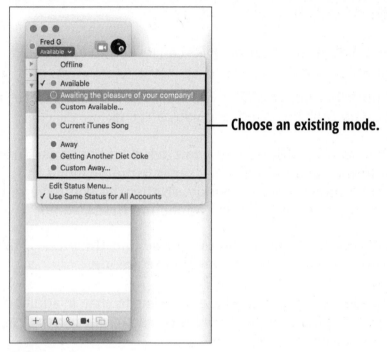

FIGURE 16-4

2. If you chose an Away mode, when you return to your computer, simply move your mouse, and Messages intelligently inquires whether you want to return to Available mode.

To create a custom status, follow these steps:

1. In the Messages Buddies window, click the Mode button below your name to display the pop-up menu.

2. Click the Custom Available or Custom Away menu entry to create the new mode.

3. In the edit box that appears, type the message you want to appear for the new mode.

4. Press Return to automatically add the newcomer to your mode list. You can also switch modes from this pop-up menu.

Chat with a Buddy

A basic text chat doesn't require a microphone or video camera on both ends; both sides of the conversation just rely on old-fashioned typing. To invite someone to a text chat, follow these steps:

1. Click the entry for that person in the Buddy List to select it.

2. Choose Buddies ⇨ Start New Chat. Messages opens a new conversation in the list on the left side of the Messages window.

Messages can also display conversations sent by others using Macs, iPhones, and iPads. These conversations are called *iMessages*, and they appear in the list as well.

3. Type your text in the entry box at the bottom of the window.

If you want to use bold or italic text, highlight the text and then press ⌘+B for Bold **(B)** or ⌘+I for Italic (*I*). You can also add an *emoji* (a symbol that conveys emotion; in techspeak, also called a *smiley*) to your text: Click the text where you want the emoji to appear, click the Smiley button to the right of the text entry field, and then choose the proper smiley from the list.

4. To send the text, press Return. Remember that you don't have to alternate sending messages back and forth between participants — you and your buddy can compose and send messages at the same time — but I like to alternate when I'm chatting.

To send a file (such as a photo or a Pages document) to someone during a chat, simply drag the file into the message area.

5. When you're done with your conversation, click the red Close button in the top-left corner of the Chat window to end the chat. You can always begin another chat session with the same buddy by clicking the conversation entry in the list and typing a new message.

Start an Audio Chat

 If the green phone icon appears next to both your name and your buddy's name in the Buddy List, you can enjoy a two-way audio (or voice) chat using an AOL, Yahoo!, Jabber, Google, or Bonjour connection.

TIP
If your Mac has a microphone hooked up, but you don't see the phone icon, choose Messages⇨Video and make sure that the Audio Chat Enabled menu item is checked.

To invite a buddy to an audio chat, follow these steps:

1. Select that person in the Buddy List.

2. Click the Start an Audio Chat button at the bottom of the Buddies window, which bears a telephone icon. An Audio Chat window opens with a Waiting for Reply message, as shown in **Figure 16-5**.

Inviting a buddy to an audio chat.

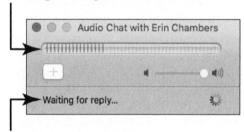

Waiting on a chat buddy.

FIGURE 16-5

3. After your buddy accepts your invitation, begin speaking. (You don't need to press a button to speak; just talk normally into the microphone.) To change the volume of your outgoing audio, drag the volume slider in the Audio Chat window to the left or right. To change the volume of your buddy's voice, drag the volume slider below that name in the Audio Chat window to the left or right. (If you're not hearing any audio after adjusting the volume, make sure that your speakers are on and that your Mac's sound isn't muted.)

4. To end your audio chat, click the red Close button in the top-left corner of the Audio Chat window.

Start a Video Chat Using Instant Messaging

When you use Messages, you can jump into a real–time, two–way video chat room, complete with audio. Both you and your buddy (or buddies) must have Apple's FaceTime camera or another brand of external web camera connected to your computers. If that's the case, you see video icons next to your buddy's name in your Buddy List (as well as next to your own name at the top of the list).

TIP

If your Mac has a microphone or video camera hooked up, but you don't see the video icon, click the Video menu and make sure that the Video Chat Enabled menu item is checked.

Starting a video chat is similar to starting an audio chat. Follow these steps:

1. Select that person in the Buddy List.

2. Click the Start a Video Chat button at the bottom of the Buddies Window (which bears a video-camera icon). Messages opens a preview window showing the live video you'll be sending.

3. If your buddy accepts the chat, a Video Chat window appears, and you can begin to talk while also seeing facial expressions, the new baby, and whatever else is going on over the video stream.

4. (Optional) Click the Effects button to choose among a range of effects for your outgoing video (such as black and white, sepia, x-ray, or thermal camera). Click a thumbnail to apply that effect to your video, or click the Original thumbnail in the middle of the display to remove all effects. When you're satisfied with the selected effect, click the Close button in the top-left corner of the Video Effects dialog to return to the Video Chat window.

5. When you're done chatting, click the red Close button in the top-left corner of the Video Chat window.

TIP

As with an audio chat, a prompt appears if you're invited to a video chat, and you can accept or decline. (You even see a video preview of the person who's inviting you.)

Converse Using FaceTime

Although the standard video chat provided by Messages is downright nifty, it has limits: You're confined to your IM buddies, and those folks may not have the necessary video hardware. With Apple's Face-Time technology, however, you can video-chat with owners of iOS devices (think iPhone, iPod touch, and iPad) and other Macs without the constraints of IM accounts. And if they can run FaceTime, they're *guaranteed* to have the right video hardware!

At this writing, FaceTime–compatible devices include Macs and iOS devices running iOS 7 or later.

You do need a Wi-Fi or cellular connection to use FaceTime with a mobile device, and your computer requires either a wired or Wi-Fi (wireless) connection to the Internet.

To launch FaceTime from within Messages, click a conversation in the list and then click the Buddies menu. If the FaceTime Video and FaceTime Audio appear on the menu, that person is capable of accepting a FaceTime call. Click the desired type of call on the Buddies menu; Messages automatically launches the FaceTime application and calls the other person.

Note that you don't need to use Messages to start a FaceTime call; you can also launch the FaceTime application separately, either from the Dock or from Launchpad. The first time you use the application, you have to enter your Apple ID (which I show you how to create in Chapter 2, as part of the Setup Assistant) and your email address. The folks you chat with on the other end use that same email address to call you via FaceTime. iPhone owners can be called via their telephone numbers.

TIP

To change the email address that other FaceTime users use to call you, choose FaceTime➪Preferences, click the Settings tab, and enable the check boxes next to the desired addresses. To add a new email address, click the Add Email button.

When you run FaceTime separately, the application displays your Recent Calls list. To initiate a call with any contact, double-click the name in the list, and the connection process begins. (You can also search your Contacts database by clicking the Enter a Name, Email or Number text box at the top of the list.)

When the call is accepted, you see a large window with a smaller "picture-in-picture" display, as shown in **Figure 16-6**. The video from the other person fills the large window, and the video that you're sending to her appears in the small display. To end the Face-Time call, click the End icon.

FIGURE 16-6

Share on a Blog (an Online Journal)

In its purest form, a *blog* is simply an online journal kept on the web by an individual or group. At least, that's what blogs started as several years ago. Most blogs are now online podiums where personal opinion is king. (Keep in mind that *anyone* can put up a blog, no matter how wildly inaccurate or biased the content may be.) You can keep up with people you know or your favorite organizations or writers if they keep a blog. The following tips help you understand what a blog is and how it works:

» A blog can contain text, photos, audio, and video.

» A blog is basically a website with a special format. You visit a blog by typing its web address in your Safari browser. Chapter 14 explains using Safari to check out websites.

» You can find blogs that focus on any topic that interests you. Politics (of course), gardening, travel, and photography are well represented on the Internet.

» Some blogs allow you to add a comment to the author's post. To do so, you typically click the Comment button or link next to that post. Just keep in mind that whatever you post is public, and everyone on the Internet can read it.

Communicate in Message Forums

Unlike a blog, a message forum is more like a conversation. Think of a series of public email messages. On a message forum, however, an original topic message leads to replies from multiple forum members. These discussions can last for weeks. (I've been part of topics that have spanned months, including dozens of replies.)

Forums are known as sources of information and recommendations on a particular topic, such as Mac troubleshooting or genealogy. I often use my favorite photography forum to gather opinions on cameras and lenses before I buy. I also enjoy reading the various tips and "spirited" conversations among professional photographers on all sorts of optical topics.

Forum message bases include various features, depending on the software used to host the forum. The forum site likely keeps track of the messages you read, enabling you to read only the new messages on the topics you choose. You likely can format your messages as you like, with color, italic, and emoticons.

Suppose that you need tips on how to fine-tune a slideshow within Photos. Follow these steps:

1. Visit Apple's Photos forums at www.apple.com/support/mac-apps/photos.

2. Click the Support Communities – Photos link to display the Photos forum page.

3. To read a discussion, click the topic line (which appears in bold blue type).

TIP

If you don't see the topic you're interested in, you can perform a search. Click the Search or Ask a Question box and type your search term. Because I'm interested in a specific Photos feature, I would type **slideshow**. Then press Return to display discussions on your particular topic, or ask a brand-new question.

Anyone can host a forum message base. Companies offer forums to allow discussions among employees, and it's easy for a club to offer a forum for its members. As with blogs, you find both free and commercial forum hosting sites by making a simple Google search at www.google.com.

Network with Others

I'll be honest: I find social networking sites such as Facebook (www.facebook.com) and Twitter (http://twitter.com) simply addictive! They make the following activities so easy:

» **Search for friends and family who are also members of the network.** The list includes old friends you lost touch with over the years. You can search for members from your hometown or high school, for example.

» **Share photos and commentary with everyone.** These services make it easy to share photos by giving you a photo page that other users can see. You can choose the images you want to share with everyone. You can also join in simple discussions with others by posting messages on their pages.

» **Play games with network contacts.** Games on a social network site are usually quick to play and involve a lot of users, so competition can be heavy on the more-popular games! Facebook, for example, offers you the chance to build your own country or engage in battles with others as a superhero.

» **Find fun activities.** I use Facebook to check on local live concerts in my area, as well as to throw virtual snowballs at others and swap favorite jokes.

» **Share your contact list.** If you know people who are your friends in real life (or who went to the same school or worked at the same company), you can recommend them to one another so that they can become friends online as well.

TIP

Both Facebook and Twitter are free to join, and you can feel safe knowing that your personal information is secure. (You should never post personal information such as your address or telephone number in your public member record, however.)

5
Taking Care of Your Computer

IN THIS PART . . .

Keeping your Mac secure from tampering

Finding and repairing problems with your Mac's drives

Updating OS X and your applications

Backing up critical files for safekeeping

Deleting unnecessary files and programs

Chapter 17

Protecting El Capitan

The wise Mac owner is aware of the security issues that surround today's computers — from the Internet and from unauthorized use directly from the keyboard!

If you're concerned that your Mac is vulnerable to attacks by Bad CyberGuys, rest assured that your computer is surrounded by defenses that you can't even see. In this chapter, you find out how to

» Protect your data and applications behind your El Capitan firewall.

» Configure FileVault to protect your hard drive.

» Configure your Mac for the tightest login security.

If some of this vocabulary is new to you, or you've heard about a firewall but aren't quite sure what one is, you're in good hands here.

Understand Computer Security

Computers now face three major security challenges:

» **Attacks from the Internet:** A *hacker* (a computer user who wants to take control of your computer) can use your Internet connection to monitor your communications or receive copies of your data.

» **Viruses:** You've probably heard of *viruses,* which are applications that can damage El Capitan or your files or slow your Mac. Although viruses are far less common on Macs than on Windows machines, you should invest in a good antivirus application to ensure that your computer remains pristine. El Capitan doesn't come with a built-in antivirus application, but I use the excellent commercial antivirus application ClamXav, available from www.clamxav.com. Another great antivirus solution — this one free — is Sophos Home, available from www.sophos.com.

» **Unauthorized users:** Whether a user is your niece at your desktop keyboard or someone who has stolen your MacBook laptop, you want to protect your private documents and prevent anyone from using your Mac without your permission.

With the right security safeguards in position, you can rest easy, knowing that your Mac is well protected.

TIP

Although you may not consider creating a backup of your Mac to be a security safeguard, it *definitely* is. With a full backup safely stored in your home or office, you're protected in case your files and data are stolen, damaged, or destroyed. Hey, life happens.

Customize the El Capitan Firewall

El Capitan's built-in software *firewall* acts as the wall surrounding your castle — I mean, your Mac — by allowing in the communications you want while preventing unknown communications from potential threats. The firewall works with your Internet connection and with any networks you may have joined.

 To display the Firewall settings, click the System Preferences icon on the Dock and then click the Security & Privacy icon. Click the Firewall tab to display the settings in **Figure 17-1**.

Select this option for your firewall.

FIGURE 17-1

If your firewall hasn't yet been turned on, click the Turn On Firewall button to start the ball rolling. (In the figure, this button has toggled to Turn Off Firewall because I already have my firewall on.)

 Is the Turn On Firewall button disabled? Don't panic; just click the padlock icon in the lower-left corner. If El Capitan prompts you for your Admin user account password, type it and then click Unlock.

TIP

Click the Firewall Options button, and El Capitan presents three options you can set (see **Figure 17-2**):

» **Block All Incoming Connections:** I recommend not using this option because turning it on reduces the data you receive, cutting off access to the Internet for virtually all your applications. (In other words, blocking *all* incoming Internet connections is overly drastic security that prevents you from doing many of the nifty things I demonstrate in this book.) Use this feature only if you suspect that your Mac is the target of an Internet hacking attack.

» **Automatically Allow Signed Software to Receive Incoming Connections:** Enable this one right now. After you do, software you've installed that's accompanied by a valid security certificate (including any application from Apple and most major third-party software developers) is automatically added to the Allowed list you see on the Firewall Options sheet. If an application without a security certificate tries to access the Internet, your Mac displays a dialog prompting you for confirmation, and you can decide yes or no.

  • You can manually add an application to the Allowed list. Click the button with the plus sign at the bottom of the list and then navigate to the application that needs to communicate with the outside world. Click the application to select it and then click Add. Remember: Only third-party applications you install yourself will likely need to be added to the Allowed list, because all the applications that Apple includes with your Mac are already on the list.

  • To delete an application from the Allowed list and return it to blocked status, select it in the list and click the button with the minus sign.

  You can edit the settings in a specific application by clicking the pop-up menu on the right side of the entry. By default, the setting is Allow Incoming Connections (including both your local network and the Internet). However, you can choose Block Incoming Connections to prevent that application from receiving any communications.

TIP

» **Enable Stealth Mode:** Here's an option that I recommend turning on. Stealth mode helps prevent hackers from attacking your Mac by preventing it from responding to simple identification queries across the Internet. Hackers often search the Internet for available computers that automatically respond to such queries.

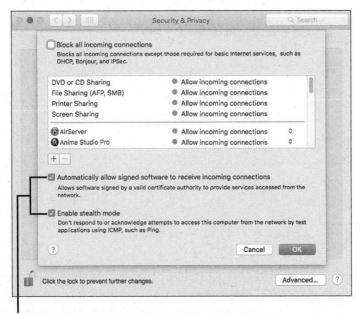

Enable these two settings for best security.

FIGURE 17-2

If you suddenly can't connect to other computers or share files that you originally could share, review the settings that you enabled on this pane: They may be the culprits. You can also verify that the correct sharing services are still enabled in the Sharing pane within System Preferences, as shown in **Figure 17-3**. (When you enable a service through the Sharing pane, El Capitan automatically adds that service to the Allowed list. When I turn on Printer Sharing on the Sharing pane, for example, El Capitan adds a Printer Sharing entry to the firewall's Allowed list.) Open the System Preferences window and click the Sharing icon, and make sure that the services you want to provide are selected.

Make sure that Sharing settings are enabled.

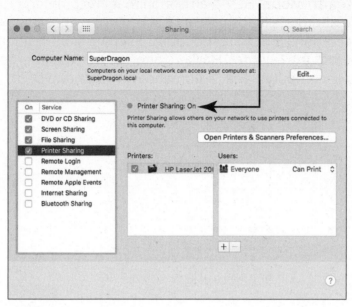

FIGURE 17-3

Configure and Run FileVault

As I mention earlier in this chapter, every Mac owner should be interested in securing personal files from prying eyes. Granted, this isn't a problem if you're the only one using your Mac. However, if you're sharing a computer with others, or your MacBook is a mobile beast, you may want a little more protection for those all-important tax records and that journal you're keeping.

Never fear: El Capitan offers the *FileVault* feature, which provides hard drive encryption that prevents just about anyone except the NSA or FBI from gaining access to the files on your hard drive. You can enable the FileVault feature on the Security & Privacy pane in System Preferences, as shown in **Figure 17-4**.

Click to turn on FileVault.

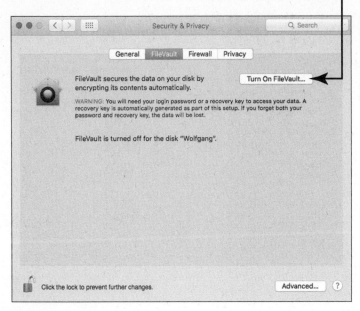

FIGURE 17-4

To configure FileVault, follow these steps:

1. Click the System Preferences icon on the Dock.

2. Click the Security & Privacy icon and then click the FileVault tab.

3. Click the Turn on FileVault button.

4. Use your iCloud account password by clicking Allow My iCloud Account to Unlock My Disk; then click Continue.

If your system has multiple user accounts, you see the Enable User sheet, shown in **Figure 17-5**.

5. Have each user click the Enable User button next to his or her entry in the list and enter his or her login password.

(FileVault uses an account's login password as the primary encryption password.)

When all accounts in the list have a check mark next to them, click Continue.

6. Click Restart to restart your Mac and begin the encryption process.

FIGURE 17-5

I love this feature, and I use it on all my Macs running El Capitan. Yet a risk is involved (insert ominous chord here). To wit: *DO NOT* forget your login password, and make doggone sure that your admin user can enter your iCloud account password!

OS X displays a dire warning for anyone who's considering using FileVault: If you forget these passwords, you can't retrieve *any* data from your Mac's hard drive. *Period.* As Jerry Reed used to say, "It's a gone pecan."

TIP

To take full advantage of an encrypted hard drive, you need to disable automatic login (as I discuss in the next section). Think about this possible security back door: On the Users & Groups pane, you've set your Mac to automatically log you in every time you boot your computer. This is the very definition of Not Secure. because your login account password automatically decrypts the FileVault data! Therefore, make sure that you actually have to log in to access your account.

Configure Secure User Options

You can configure El Capitan for tighter login security, making it much harder for anyone to sit down at your Mac and break into your system. The secure login options are located on the System Preferences Security & Privacy pane, so click the System Preferences icon on the Dock and then click the Security & Privacy icon. Click the General tab to display the settings in **Figure 17-6**.

Select these security options.

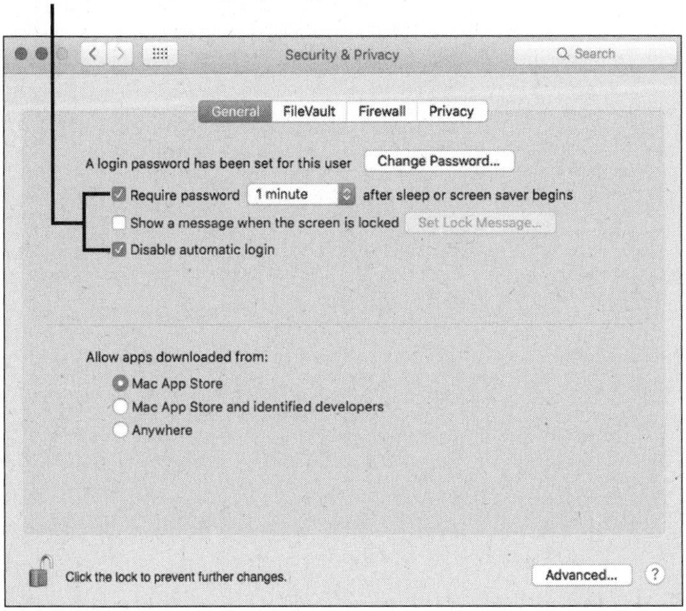

FIGURE 17-6

For tighter security, I recommend that you enable these options:

» **Require Password <*time*> After Sleep or Screen Saver Begins:**
Select this option to add an extra layer of password security to a laptop (or a Mac in a public area). OS X El Capitan then requires that you enter your login password before the system returns from a sleep state or exits a screen saver. The pop-up menu specifies the amount of time that must pass before your password is required.

» **Disable Automatic Login:** Enable this option to force a full login every time you boot your Mac. (Laptop owners, take note: Turn on this option to prevent a thief from accessing your data!) As I mention in the preceding section, you should also disable automatic login if you're using FileVault encryption.

» **Allow Apps Downloaded From:** Click the Mac App Store radio button to select it, which prevents any application that has not been checked and approved by Apple from running on your Mac.

Chapter 18

Maintaining Your Mac

Although your Mac doesn't roam the highway like your car does, a computer still needs regular maintenance. Over time, regular use (and unexpected events, such as power outages) can produce problems ranging from hard drive errors to slower browser performance.

Don't worry — there's no oil filter to change! In this chapter, you find out how to

» Detect and correct errors in your Mac's file system.

» Automatically download and install the latest updates for OS X El Capitan.

» Back up your important files and folders with an inexpensive USB flash drive.

» Trim those unnecessary and outdated files from your drive to reclaim space.

Scan a Drive for Errors

El Capitan's Disk Utility is a handy tool for troubleshooting and repairing your hard drive (whether you're noticing that your Mac has slowed considerably or you have problems opening files and applications). You can find it in the Utilities folder within the Applications folder. From Launchpad, click the Utilities folder and then click the Disk Utility icon.

In the left column of the Disk Utility window, you can see

TIP

» The *physical* hard drives in your system (the actual hardware)

» The *volumes* (the data stored on the hard drives)

You can always tell a volume, because it's indented below the physical drive entry.

» Any CD or DVD loaded on your Mac

» External USB or Thunderbolt hard drives

» USB flash drives

Flash drives (like thumb drives) are external hardware devices that you can add to your Mac for additional storage room or as secure places to back up your data.

In **Figure 18-1**, I have one internal hard drive (the 1TB SATA entry, which is selected) and one USB external hard drive (the Toshiba entry). The hard drive has three volumes (Wolfgang, Ludwig, and Johann), and the USB drive has one volume (Time Machine).

Disk Utility also fixes incorrect file *permissions* automatically. Files with corrupt or incorrect permissions can

» Make your Mac lock up

» Make applications act goofy (or refuse to run)

» Cause strange behavior within a Finder window or System Preferences

Physical hard drive

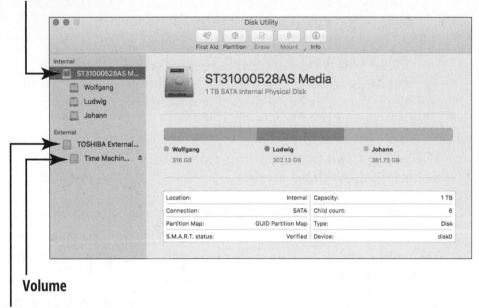

Volume

External USB hard drive

FIGURE 18-1

Using Disk Utility to repair your hard drive carries a couple of caveats:

» **You can't repair the boot disk or the boot volume if OS X won't run.** This statement makes sense because Disk Utility is launched from your boot volume. (The *boot volume* is usually your Mac's internal hard drive, where El Capitan is installed.) If OS X isn't booting completely or is locking up, you can't launch Disk Utility.

To repair your boot hard drive if OS X isn't running, you need to boot your Mac from El Capitan's Recovery HD volume. Hold down the Option key immediately after you hear the start-up chord to display the Mac OS X boot menu, and choose the Recovery HD volume. When the Recovery window appears, run Disk Utility. Because you've booted the system from the Recovery HD volume, you can repair problems with your start-up hard drive.

Select your boot hard drive or volume in the sidebar at the left, and the First Aid button should be enabled.

> » **You can't repair CDs and DVDs.** Because CDs and DVDs are read-only media, they can't be repaired (at least not by Disk Utility).
>
> If your Mac is having trouble reading a CD or DVD, wipe the disc with a soft cloth to remove dust, oil, and fingerprints. If that technique fails, invest in a disc-cleaning contrivance of some sort. Look for a CD/DVD cleaning kit.

If OS X El Capitan is running fine, and you need to repair a disk or volume, follow these steps:

1. Save all open documents, and quit all running applications.

2. Click the Spotlight search icon on the Finder menu bar, type **Disk Utility**, and press Return. (From within Launchpad, click the Utilities folder and then click the Disk Utility icon.)

3. In the list on the left side of the Disk Utility window, click the disk or volume that you want to check.

4. Click the First Aid button and then click Run to confirm.

If Disk Utility does indeed find errors, they'll be fixed automatically. Would you expect anything less from our favorite operating system?

Keep El Capitan Up to Date

Apple releases all sorts of updates for El Capitan, and it's important to apply these updates as soon as possible. Some updates fix obvious problems in OS X, whereas other changes are made behind the scenes (including security updates to help guard against all sorts of malicious attacks through the Internet).

You can set your Mac to automatically download and update your system with these OS X updates. To configure automatic updates, follow these steps:

 1. Click the System Preferences icon on the Dock.

2. Click the App Store icon to display the settings you see in **Figure 18-2**.

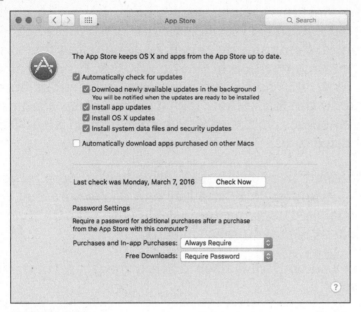

The App Store keeps OS X and apps from the App Store up to date.

☑ Automatically check for updates
  ☑ Download newly available updates in the background
     You will be notified when the updates are ready to be installed
  ☑ Install app updates
  ☑ Install OS X updates
  ☑ Install system data files and security updates

☐ Automatically download apps purchased on other Macs

Last check was Monday, March 7, 2016   Check Now

Password Settings

Require a password for additional purchases after a purchase from the App Store with this computer?

Purchases and In-app Purchases: Always Require
Free Downloads: Require Password

FIGURE 18-2

3. Click the Automatically Check for Updates check box to enable it, as well as the four check boxes below it.

4. Press ⌘+Q (or click the Close button in the top-left corner of the System Preferences window) to exit System Preferences and save your changes.

Back Up Important Files and Folders

Have you ever accidentally deleted a file or folder that was very important to you, such as your genealogy data files or your Great American Novel in progress? It's truly a painful experience. You can avoid that heartache with an inexpensive USB flash drive and a little preparation!

I call this process a "down and dirty" backup because it doesn't protect your entire system automatically, the way El Capitan's built-in Time Machine backup system does. It's much cheaper than buying an external 1TB USB hard drive, however, and no setup is involved. Computer owners have been using this simple trick ever since the invention of the floppy disk. If you do decide to use Time Machine, you'll find complete instructions on setting things up in the El Capitan Help system (which I discuss in Chapter 7). Remember, you need to buy an external USB or Thunderbolt hard drive to use Time Machine!

If you don't already have a USB flash drive handy, drop by your local electronics or computer store and buy one. Make sure that the drive you choose is labeled as being compatible with Mac OS X and that it provides at least 32GB of storage capacity.

Then you can use your USB flash drive to back up your important files, as follows:

1. Plug the drive into your Mac's USB port.

   The drive should appear on your Desktop and in the Devices section on the left side of any Finder window.

2. Drag the files you want to back up to the USB drive icon in either location.

   You can drag one file at a time or an entire folder's worth of files.

   With a "down and dirty" backup, you're copying only those files that you *absolutely* can't afford to lose. Before I travel, I typically open my Documents folder on my MacBook and copy the files I'll use on the trip to my USB drive. Even if my MacBook is lost or stolen, I'll still have that USB backup in my pocket or suitcase.

3. When you're done copying files, eject the flash drive by right-clicking the flash drive's icon and choosing Eject from the pop-up menu.

Store that drive in a safe location. Repeat the process again as necessary to "freshen" your backup files.

Restoring a file is as easy as plugging in the flash drive and copying the files back to your Mac's hard drive.

TIP

Have you created an Apple ID/iCloud account? If so, it's also possible to back up those same essential files to your iCloud Drive instead of a USB flash drive. Instead of dragging the files to an external drive, drag them to the iCloud Drive entry at the left side of the Finder window. I should, however, mention two caveats with iCloud Drive storage: first, there's a set limit to the total capacity of your iCloud Drive (typically less than 5GB). Also, if you're unable to log in to your iCloud account — either on your Mac or another person's Mac — you can't access those files.

Remove Unnecessary Files

If you're running low on drive space (and you've already deleted any unneeded downloads), it may be time to consider deleting "old" applications to reclaim some space! By contrast with Windows 10, OS X doesn't have a stand-alone utility for uninstalling software. It doesn't need one, because virtually all Macintosh applications are self-contained in a single folder or series of nested folders.

Because of this rule, removing an application is *usually* as easy as deleting the contents of the installation folder from your hard drive (removing the Quicken folder to uninstall Quicken, for example). You find the application's installation folder within your Application folder. Choose Go⇨Applications (or press ⌘+Shift+A) to jump there directly.

But don't delete that folder immediately. Take a second to check the application's README file (which usually has the oh-so subtle filename README) and documentation for any special instructions before you delete any application's folder! If you've created any documents in that folder that you want to keep — maybe you plan to reinstall the application later — don't forget to move them before you send the folder and its contents to the Trash. In fact, some applications come complete with their own uninstall utility, so checking the README file and documentation may save you unnecessary steps.

Index

M

N

USB scanner, 124
Usenet group (newsgroup), 227

V

Verisign, 244
versions (software), 12
video, buying from iTunes Store, 196–199
video chats (Messages app), 281–282
VirusBarrier X8 app, 225
viruses
  in email attachments, 225, 262
  protecting against, 290
  in removable media, 225
  from web downloads, 224
visual alerts/notifications, 92–93
visualizations (iTunes), 196
voice technical support, 132
volume control (iTunes), 188–189
volumes (hard drive), 300

W

web browsing, 232–234. *See also* Safari
web discussion groups, 128–129, 284–285

web pages, printing, 247
WebSense, 244
websites
  secure, 234
  visiting, 230–232
widgets, 48, 59–60
windows
  defined, 50
  minimizing and restoring, 72
  moving and resizing, 73–74
  opening, 68
  scrolling, 70–71
  switching, 69–70
  title bar, 73
  zooming, 72–73
wireless Internet connection, 217–218

Y

Year view (Photo app), 171

Z

Zoom feature (Safari), 231–232
zooming windows, 72–73

About the Author

Mark L. Chambers has been an author, computer consultant, BBS sysop, programmer, and hardware technician for more than 30 years — pushing computers and their uses far beyond "normal" performance limits for decades now. His first love affair with a computer peripheral blossomed in 1984, when he bought his lightning-fast 300-bps modem for his Atari 400. Now he spends entirely too much time on the Internet and drinks far too much caffeine-laden soda.

With a degree in journalism and creative writing from Louisiana State University, Mark took the logical career choice: programming computers. After five years as a COBOL programmer for a hospital system, however, he decided that there must be a better way to earn a living, and he became the documentation manager for Datastorm Technologies, a well-known communications software developer. Somewhere between designing and writing software manuals, Mark began writing computer how-to books. His first book, *Running a Perfect BBS*, was published in 1994. After 20 years of fun (disguised as hard work), Mark is one of the most productive and best-selling technology authors on the planet.

Along with writing several books a year and editing whatever his publishers throw at him, Mark has branched out into web-based education, designing and teaching online classes.

His favorite pastimes include collecting gargoyles, watching St. Louis Cardinals baseball, playing his three pinball machines and the latest computer games, supercharging computers, and rendering 3D flights of fancy. During all that activity, he listens to just about every type of music imaginable. Mark's worldwide Internet radio station, MLC Radio (at www.mlcbooks.com), plays only CD-quality classics from 1970 to 1979, including everything from Rush to Billy Joel to the *Rocky Horror Picture Show* soundtrack.

Mark's rapidly expanding list of books includes *MacBook For Dummies*, 6th Edition; *iMac For Dummies*, 9th Edition; *Mac OS X Yosemite All-in-One For Dummies*; *PCs All-in-One For Dummies*, 6th Edition; *Build Your Own PC Do-It-Yourself For Dummies*; *Scanners For Dummies*, 2nd Edition; *CD & DVD Recording For Dummies*, 2nd Edition; *Mac OS X Tiger: Top*

100 Simplified Tips & Tricks; *Hewlett-Packard Official Printer Handbook*; *Hewlett-Packard Official Recordable CD Handbook*; *Digital Photography Handbook*; *Computer Gamer's Bible*; *Recordable CD Bible*; *Teach Yourself Visually iMac* (all from John Wiley & Sons); *Running a Perfect BBS*; *Official Netscape Guide to Web Animation*; *Windows 98 Optimizing and Troubleshooting Little Black Book*; *Microsoft Office v. X for Mac Power User's Guide*; and *Burn It! Creating Your Own Great DVDs and CDs*.

Mark's books have been translated into 16 languages so far; his favorites are German, Polish, Dutch, and French. Although he can't read them, he enjoys the pictures immensely.

Mark welcomes all comments about his books. You can reach him at MLC Books Online, his website, at www.mlcbooks.com.

Dedication

This book is proudly dedicated to my Uncle Tuffy and my Aunt Ruby — a couple forever young and forever in love.

Publisher's Acknowledgments

Acquisitions Editor: Amy Fandrei

Project Editor: Charlotte Kughen

Copy Editor: Kathy Simpson

Technical Editor: Ryan Williams

Editorial Assistant: Matthew Lowe

Sr. Editorial Assistant: Cherie Case

Production Editor: Selvakumaran Rajendiran

Cover Image: © Charts and BG/Shutterstock